Autodesk® Inventor® 2017 (R2) Update for 2015/2016 Users

Student Guide

Mixed Units - 1ˢᵗ Edition

AUTODESK. Authorized Publisher

ASCENT - Center for Technical Knowledge®
Autodesk® Inventor® 2017 (R2)
Update for 2015/2016 Users
Mixed Units - 1st Edition

Prepared and produced by:

ASCENT Center for Technical Knowledge
630 Peter Jefferson Parkway, Suite 175
Charlottesville, VA 22911

866-527-2368
www.ASCENTed.com

Lead Contributor: Jennifer MacMillan

ASCENT - Center for Technical Knowledge is a division of Rand Worldwide, Inc., providing custom developed knowledge products and services for leading engineering software applications. ASCENT is focused on specializing in the creation of education programs that incorporate the best of classroom learning and technology-based training offerings.

We welcome any comments you may have regarding this student guide, or any of our products. To contact us please email: feedback@ASCENTed.com.

The following are registered trademarks or trademarks of Autodesk, Inc., and/or its subsidiaries and/or affiliates in the USA and other countries: 123D, 3ds Max, Alias, ATC, AutoCAD LT, AutoCAD, Autodesk, the Autodesk logo, Autodesk 123D, Autodesk Homestyler, Autodesk Inventor, Autodesk MapGuide, Autodesk Streamline, AutoLISP, AutoSketch, AutoSnap, AutoTrack, Backburner, Backdraft, Beast, BIM 360, Burn, Buzzsaw, CADmep, CAiCE, CAMduct, Civil 3D, Combustion, Communication Specification, Configurator 360, Constructware, Content Explorer, Creative Bridge, Dancing Baby (image), DesignCenter, DesignKids, DesignStudio, Discreet, DWF, DWG, DWG (design/logo), DWG Extreme, DWG TrueConvert, DWG TrueView, DWGX, DXF, Ecotect, Ember, ESTmep, FABmep, Face Robot, FBX, Fempro, Fire, Flame, Flare, Flint, ForceEffect, FormIt 360, Freewheel, Fusion 360, Glue, Green Building Studio, Heidi, Homestyler, HumanIK, i-drop, ImageModeler, Incinerator, Inferno, InfraWorks, Instructables, Instructables (stylized robot design/logo), Inventor, Inventor HSM, Inventor LT, Lustre, Maya, Maya LT, MIMI, Mockup 360, Moldflow Plastics Advisers, Moldflow Plastics Insight, Moldflow, Moondust, MotionBuilder, Movimento, MPA (design/logo), MPA, MPI (design/logo), MPX (design/logo), MPX, Mudbox, Navisworks, ObjectARX, ObjectDBX, Opticore, P9, Pier 9, Pixlr, Pixlr-o-matic, Productstream, Publisher 360, RasterDWG, RealDWG, ReCap, ReCap 360, Remote, Revit LT, Revit, RiverCAD, Robot, Scaleform, Showcase, Showcase 360, SketchBook, Smoke, Socialcam, Softimage, Spark & Design, Spark Logo, Sparks, SteeringWheels, Stitcher, Stone, StormNET, TinkerBox, Tinkercad, Tinkerplay, ToolClip, Topobase, Toxik, TrustedDWG, T-Splines, ViewCube, Visual LISP, Visual, VRED, Wire, Wiretap, WiretapCentral, XSI.

NASTRAN is a registered trademark of the National Aeronautics Space Administration.

All other brand names, product names, or trademarks belong to their respective holders.

General Disclaimer:

Notwithstanding any language to the contrary, nothing contained herein constitutes nor is intended to constitute an offer, inducement, promise, or contract of any kind. The data contained herein is for informational purposes only and is not represented to be error free. ASCENT, its agents and employees, expressly disclaim any liability for any damages, losses or other expenses arising in connection with the use of its materials or in connection with any failure of performance, error, omission even if ASCENT, or its representatives, are advised of the possibility of such damages, losses or other expenses. No consequential damages can be sought against ASCENT or Rand Worldwide, Inc. for the use of these materials by any third parties or for any direct or indirect result of that use.

The information contained herein is intended to be of general interest to you and is provided "as is", and it does not address the circumstances of any particular individual or entity. Nothing herein constitutes professional advice, nor does it constitute a comprehensive or complete statement of the issues discussed thereto. ASCENT does not warrant that the document or information will be error free or will meet any particular criteria of performance or quality. In particular (but without limitation) information may be rendered inaccurate by changes made to the subject of the materials (i.e. applicable software). Rand Worldwide, Inc. specifically disclaims any warranty, either expressed or implied, including the warranty of fitness for a particular purpose.

AS-INV1702-UPD1MU-SG   //   IS-INV1702-UPD1MU-SG

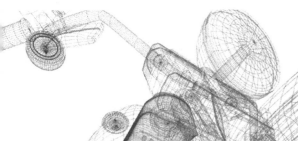

Contents

Preface

The *Autodesk® Inventor® 2017 (R2) Update for 2015/2016 Users* student guide introduces the new concepts and modeling techniques that have been added to the 2016 and 2017 releases of the Autodesk® Inventor® software. The student guide covers enhancements to the most commonly used environments and contains practices for applying the new concepts. It was written to run in the (R2) release of Autodesk Inventor 2017.

Topics Covered:

*   Interface Enhancements

*   Sketching Enhancements

*   Part Modeling Enhancements

*   Assembly Enhancements

*   Drawing Enhancements

*   Working with Presentations

*   Working with Imported Geometry

*   Generative Shape Design

*   Sheet Metal Enhancements

*   Inventor Studio Enhancements

The student guide begins with changes to the overall interface and enhancements that cover settings that pertain to multiple environments. Chapter 2 covers the sketch environment and contains many topics that have been added to ease sketch creation for both 2D and 3D sketches.

A number of enhancements have been added to existing and new part modeling tools, which is covered in Chapter 3. Changes have been made to existing features (such extrude, drafts, iFeatures), boundary patch geometry, and a new ruled surface tool. Additionally, the new tools and enhancements for patterning are discussed.

Chapters 4, 5, and 6 cover changes to the assembly, drawing, and presentation environments. Few changes were made in the assembly environment; however, the new presentation workflow is explained. The enhancements to the drawing environment will improve drawing creation, as well as how many annotations are created or are modified in a drawing.

Chapters 7 and 8 chapters cover new tools for working with imported data and the new Generative Shape Design tool.

The appendices outline changes made in the Sheet Metal environment (including multi-body sheet metal modeling) and the Inventor Studio environment.

Note on Software Setup

This student guide assumes a standard installation of the software using the default preferences during installation. Lectures and practices use the standard software templates and default options for the Content Libraries.

Students and Educators can Access Free Autodesk Software and Resources

Autodesk challenges you to get started with free educational licenses for professional software and creativity apps used by millions of architects, engineers, designers, and hobbyists today. Bring Autodesk software into your classroom, studio, or workshop to learn, teach, and explore real-world design challenges the way professionals do.

Get started today - register at the Autodesk Education Community and download one of the many Autodesk software applications available.

Visit www.autodesk.com/joinedu/

Note: Free products are subject to the terms and conditions of the end-user license and services agreement that accompanies the software. The software is for personal use for education purposes and is not intended for classroom or lab use.

Lead Contributor: Jennifer MacMillan

With a dedication for engineering and education, Jennifer has spent over 20 years at ASCENT managing courseware development for various CAD products. Trained in Instructional Design, Jennifer uses her skills to develop instructor-led and web-based training products as well as knowledge profiling tools.

Jennifer has achieved the Autodesk Certified Professional certification for Inventor and is also recognized as an Autodesk Certified Instructor (ACI). She enjoys teaching the training courses that she authors and is also very skilled in providing technical support to end-users.

Jennifer holds a Bachelor of Engineering Degree as well as a Bachelor of Science in Mathematics from Dalhousie University, Nova Scotia, Canada.

Jennifer MacMillan has been the Lead Contributor for *Autodesk Inventor Update* student guides since 2007.

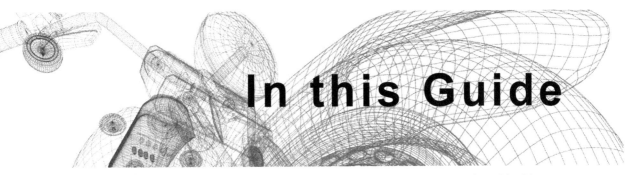

In this Guide

The following images highlight some of the features that can be found in this Student Guide.

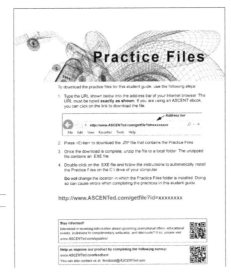

Practice Files

The Practice Files page tells you how to download and install the practice files that are provided with this student guide.

FTP link for practice files
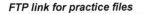

Chapters

Each chapter begins with a brief introduction and a list of the chapter's Learning Objectives.

Learning Objectives for the chapter

Instructional Content

Each chapter is split into a series of sections of instructional content on specific topics. These lectures include the descriptions, step-by-step procedures, figures, hints, and information you need to achieve the chapter's Learning Objectives.

Side notes

Side notes are hints or additional information for the current topic.

Practice Objectives

Practices

Practices enable you to use the software to perform a hands-on review of a topic.

Some practices require you to use prepared practice files, which can be downloaded from the link found on the Practice Files page.

Chapter Review Questions

Chapter review questions, located at the end of each chapter, enable you to review the key concepts and learning objectives of the chapter.

Practice Files

To download the practice files for this student guide, use the following steps:

1. Type the URL shown below into the address bar of your Internet browser. The URL must be typed **exactly as shown**. If you are using an ASCENT ebook, you can click on the link to download the file.

2. Press <Enter> to download the .ZIP file that contains the Practice Files.

3. Once the download is complete, unzip the file to a local folder. The unzipped file contains an .EXE file.

4. Double-click on the .EXE file and follow the instructions to automatically install the Practice Files on the C:\ drive of your computer.

   Do not change the location in which the Practice Files folder is installed. Doing so can cause errors when completing the practices in this student guide.

http://www.ascented.com/getfile?id=sphyraena

Stay Informed!

Interested in receiving information about upcoming promotional offers, educational events, invitations to complimentary webcasts, and discounts? If so, please visit:

www.ASCENTed.com/updates/

Help us improve our product by completing the following survey:

www.ASCENTed.com/feedback

You can also contact us at: *feedback@ASCENTed.com*

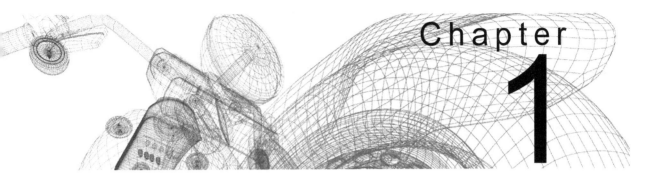

Interface and General Enhancements

In this chapter, you learn about the general enhancements that have been made to the Autodesk® Inventor® software in 2016 and 2017 (R1 and R2). The chapter focuses on the interface and the general enhancements that can improve your experience using the software.

Learning Objectives in this Chapter

- Describe the changes to the software interface.
- Describe the general changes to the default part template and the application options.
- Create a 3D PDF file.

1.1 Interface Enhancements

When you launch the Autodesk Inventor software, the My Home dashboard and *Getting Started* tab display, as shown in Figure 1–1. The changes made to the layout in these areas of the interface are further described below.

Figure 1–1

My Home

The My Home layout was initially introduced in the 2016 version of the software and small changes have been made over the past few releases.

- The default view for My Home is the Home dashboard, which displays the *New*, *Projects*, *Shortcuts*, *File Details*, and *Recent Documents* areas. The display of these sections has been streamlined since 2015 to facilitate its use. For example, a search tool is available in the *Recent Documents* area to find files and when you hover the cursor over a recent document you can open the file, remove it from the list, or access other useful options.

Ribbon

- The *Get Started* tab is now customizable so that panels can be toggled on and off, as required. By default, the Windows panel is now toggled off. This can be enabled ( ) to customize the user interface, tile windows, etc.

- In the ribbon, a **File** menu (as shown in Figure 1–2) has been added to replace the Applications Menu.

Application Menu replaced with the File menu.

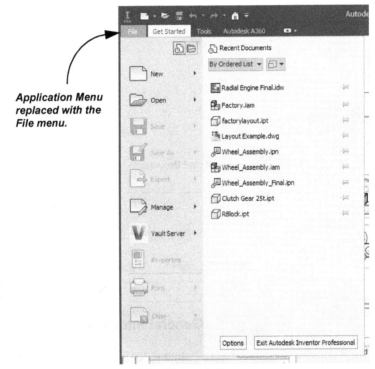

Figure 1–2

The interface for the Autodesk Inventor 2017 software has not changed substantially with recent releases of the software. The following elements have been added or enhanced in 2016. Figure 1–3 shows the interface for Autodesk Inventor 2017 (R2).

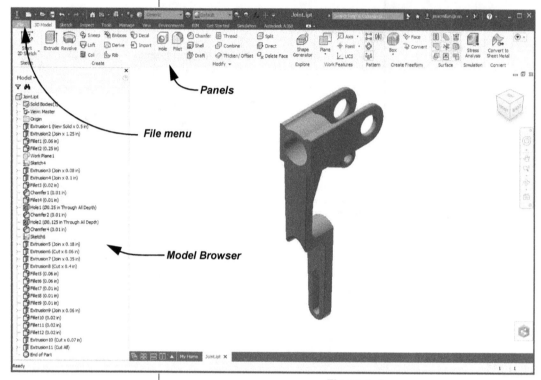

Panels

File menu

Model Browser

Figure 1–3

General Interface

- In the 2015 version of the software, many commands in the Create and Modify panels in the *3D Model* tab were grouped with other similar commands. This change has been reverted back to the layout that was previously used in the 2014 release of the software.

- The list of panels that display by default, has been reduced.

  To customize the panels that display, expand ⊙ ⁻ (Show panels) at the end of each tab and select the required panels from the available list.

- As of 2016, there are now additional tile styles listed at the bottom of the graphics window. Generally, maximizing each window provides the most modeling space, but you can also minimize and resize the windows or use  (Cascade), (Arrange), (Tile Horizontally), and (Tile Vertically), as shown in Figure 1–4.

Figure 1–4

Model Browser

- The display of expandable nodes in the Model Browser have been updated to simplify their appearance. Dashed lines are included between the nodes to easily show their hierarchy.

- You can now rename a node in your Model Browser by selecting it and pressing <F2>. This is consistent with how files are renamed in Windows.

- To quickly toggle between the available Browser displays (Model, Favorites, and Vault, as shown in Figure 1–5) you can now use <Alt> + A to toggle forward through the list or <Alt> + S to toggle backwards through the list.

Figure 1–5

Mini-Toolbar

- With the release of the Inventor 2017 (R2) software, you can now toggle off the display of the mini-toolbar. By disabling the mini-toolbar display in the User Interface drop-down list (as shown in Figure 1–6), commands as such as **Extrude**, **Revolve**, **Fillet**, **Shell**, **Draft**, **Chamfer**, and **Joints**, use the dialog box for feature creation.

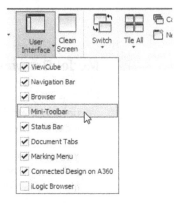

Figure 1–6

Quick Access Toolbar

- The **Undo** and **Redo** commands in the Quick Access Toolbar have been enhanced in the (R2) release of the 2017 software to visually display the list of actions that can be undone or redone. By selecting a previous action in the list (as shown in Figure 1–7) you can return directly to that point in the design history.

Figure 1–7

Model Display

- The lighting style interface in the Style and Standard Editor has been streamlined so that all the options for defining the lighting style are now divided into multiple tabs, as shown in Figure 1–8. Additionally, the Environment (☼) and Standard Lighting (♀) styles are now identified using icons in the dialog box.

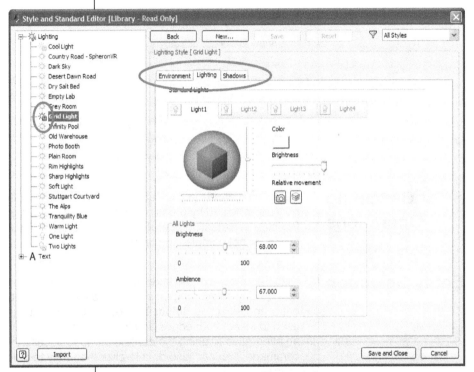

Figure 1–8

- The Visual Style setting for new part models is now set as **Shaded with Edges**. Prior to 2016, this option was set to **Shaded**.

1.2 General Enhancements

Part Template File

As of 2017, models created with a default template display as Isometric and contain three additional default Design Views, as shown in Figure 1–9. Each of these new views reorients the model. Prior to 2017, only a Master Design View was provided.

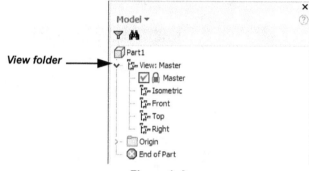

Figure 1–9

Canceling Operations

Select commands in the Autodesk Inventor 2016 software can now be canceled by pressing <Esc>. This provides greater flexibility in canceling operations that are either executed in error, failing, or not completing correctly.

Entity Selection

With the release of the Inventor 2017 (R2) software, you can now quickly select tangent entities in a model by right-clicking an entity and selecting **Select Tangencies**. This new option can be used to select both edges and faces, as shown Figure 1–10. As an alternative to using the context menu to access the command, you can also double-click the entity to quickly select all tangent entities.

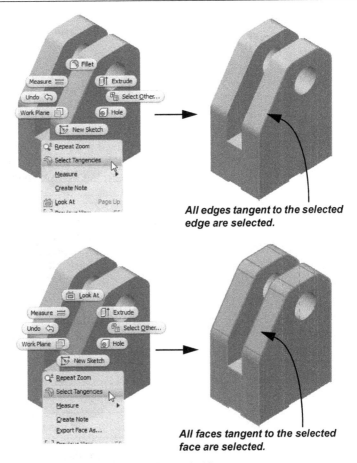

All edges tangent to the selected edge are selected.

All faces tangent to the selected face are selected.

Figure 1–10

iLogic Enhancement

With the release of the Inventor 2017 (R2) software, the Edit Rule dialog box was updated to provide a new **Save** and **Save & Run** option, as shown in Figure 1–11. These commands replace the **OK** option previously available. With this change, it is now possible to save the rule without running it using the **Save** option or to save the rule and subsequently run it using the **Save & Run** option.

Figure 1–11

Application Options

The following changes have been made to the tabs in the Application Options dialog box:

- On the *Save* tab, you can specify how the file will handle the translation report for files that are being imported. Prior to 2016, the report was saved as an external file. Now you can select whether to embed the report in the document, save it externally, or not create one at all.

- On the *File* tab, you can now set a default *Sketch Symbol Library* folder to be used when working with symbols. Additionally, the *File Open* options have been regrouped into one area.

- **Disable Automatic Refinement** is a new Application Option in 2017 that can be found in the *Display* tab. This controls the faceting in both large assemblies and complex model geometry and is discussed in the *Assembly Enhancement* chapter.

- As of 2016, a new command has been added to the *Part* tab that enables you to use the color override from a source component when deriving geometry. This option is enabled by default.

- A new *My Home* area is now available in the *General* tab. It controls whether My Home displays on startup and controls the number of recent documents that display. The default number is 50, and the maximum is 200.

- As of 2017, two new options have been added on the *Sketch* tab. They enable you to set linking as the default option when an image in imported and control the opacity of a sketch through a shaded model.

File Import & Export

The Inventor 2017 software is now able to export models as 3D PDF by clicking **File>Export>3D PDF**. The exported 3D PDF is created using a default template; however, a custom template can be created and used, as required. Once created, it can be viewed in Adobe Acrobat Reader, similar to that shown in Figure 1–12. Available tools enable you to select design view representations, model properties, and attachments to include.

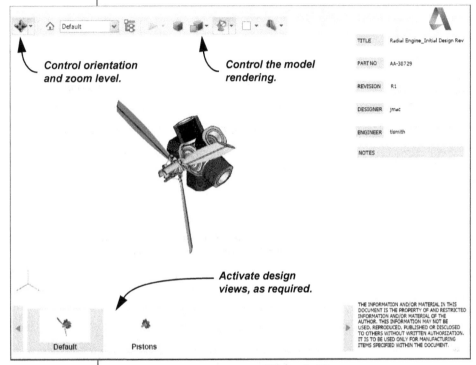

Figure 1–12

- Expanded version support is introduced with new releases, aiming to improve interoperability in Inventor. For a complete list of the changes, refer to the Help and search on "Translators Enhancements".

Chapter Review Questions

1. The My Home dashboard can be used to set project files, create new files, access recently opened files, and open new files.

   a. True

   b. False

2. What does the at the end of the tabs on the ribbon enable you to do?

   a. Toggle the display of commands on/off in the ribbon.

   b. Toggle the display of panels on/off in the ribbon.

   c. Toggle the display of tabs on/off in the ribbon.

3. To access the **3D PDF** command, you must use the **Export** option in the Application Menu.

   a. True

   b. False

4. Match the following icons in the graphics window to their window customization option.

   a. Tile Horizontally   _____

   b. Cascade   _____

   c. Tile Vertically   _____

   d. Arrange   _____

5. Which of the following shortcut keys can be used in the Model Browser to rename a feature?

   a. <Alt> + A

   b. <Alt> + S

   c. <F6>

   d. <F2>

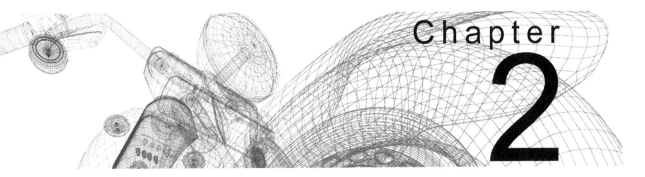

Chapter 2

Sketching Enhancements

In this chapter, you learn about the enhancements that have been made to the 2D and 3D sketching environments.

Learning Objectives in this Chapter

- Describe the new and enhanced sketching tools in the 2D sketch environment.
- Describe the new and enhanced Draw tools in the 2D sketch environment.
- Describe the sketch tools in the Status Bar in a 3D sketch.
- Realign the sketch triad in a 3D sketch.
- Modify 3D sketch entities using the 3D Transform command.
- Constrain 3D sketch entities using the constraint options introduced in 2017.

2.1 General Sketching Tool Enhancements

The following sketch creation or editing tools have been added or changed in the Autodesk® Inventor® software:

Show and Hide Constraints

Prior to 2016, when the **Show All Constraints** option was enabled in a sketch, all constraint symbols for the current sketched entities would display. When additional entities were sketched, their constraint symbols would not automatically display unless **Show All Constraints** was selected again. As of 2016, once this option is enabled, it continuously displays constraints for any additional entities until **Hide All Constraints** is selected. Both of these options are available in the right-click context menu, as shown in Figure 2–1.

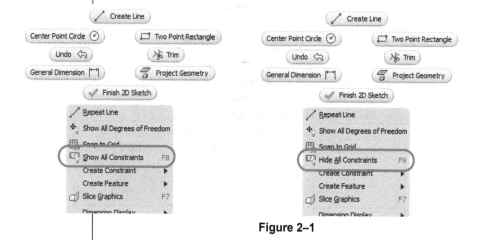

Figure 2–1

Sketched Text

When adding text to a sketch, the Format Text dialog box has been updated to provide additional text formatting tools, as shown in Figure 2–2. The new functionality was introduced in 2016 and includes the following:

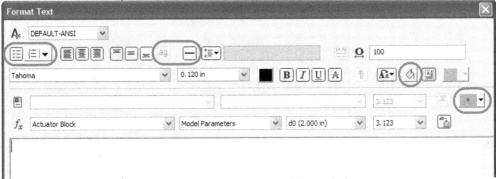

Figure 2–2

To create a custom text style that can be used in other sketches, you can use the Style and Standard Editor to create a new style.

- Bullets, numbering, and strike-through can be used to format text. When bullets or numbers are copied from Word, the formatting is still recognized.

- Justification to the baseline of the text box when using the **Single Line Text** option.

- Text can be modified to be all caps, title case, or lower case once the text has been added.

- Enhanced symbol list has been included.

- A background fill color can be added to the text box. (This is new in 2017).

- The Zoom In and Zoom Out controls for enlarging the text in the text area have been removed. To change the text display size, place the cursor in the text area, hold <Ctrl>, and use the scroll wheel on your mouse to zoom.

Snap Points

Snap points enable you to locate the entity points by snapping to points of existing entities in a sketch. As of 2016, the **Point Snaps** options were expanded to include additional options, as shown in Figure 2–3.

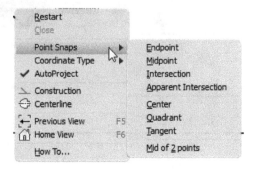

Figure 2–3

Sketch Visibility

As of 2016, you can now clear the display of dimensions from all sketches in the model at once by selecting the **Sketch Dimensions** Object visibility setting (*View* tab>Visibility panel).

Show Input

Once a sketch is created, you can now easily investigate the sketch plane that was used to create the sketch. To display the source sketch plane for a sketch, right-click on the sketch and select **Show Input**. This is available in Inventor 2016 or greater.

Share Sketch

When consumed sketches are shared by dragging and dropping it above its parent feature, they are now automatically set as visible. Prior to 2016, using the drag technique did not automatically set the shared sketch as visible.

Dimensions

It is now possible to assign two tangent dimensions between circular/arc entities to fully constrain a sketch, as shown in Figure 2–4. When placing dimensions, you must select in the required quadrant of the arc and ensure that the ⌀ glyph displays before placing the dimension. Prior to 2016, this was not possible and a diameter or radial dimension would have been required to fully constrain the sketch.

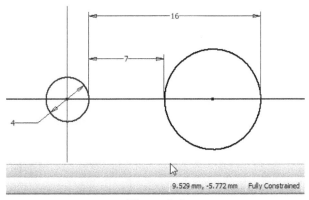

Figure 2–4

Exporting a Sketch as a DWG File

Any part or assembly sketches can now be exported with the same properties specified in the Geometry Properties dialog box. Prior to Inventor 2017 (R2), the properties were not exported and the DWG file was exported as solid lines regardless of the style assigned in the sketch.

2.2 3D Sketch Enhancements

A number of changes were introduced for 3D sketches with the release of Inventor 2016 and 2017. The *3D Sketch* tab now includes a number of new and enhanced tools for creating 3D sketch geometry, constraining sketches, and transforming a sketch. The following summarizes these changes.

Project to Surface

As of 2016, The **Wrap to Surface** *Output* option (as shown in Figure 2–5) in the **Project to Surface** ( ) tool has been enhanced so that multiple types of surfaces (planar and curved) can be selected at the same time. With this enhancement, you will experience more predictable results using this command.

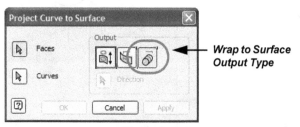

Figure 2–5

Silhouette Curves

A silhouette curve represents the contour of the model relative to a specific pull direction. Prior to 2016, you had no control over which curves were created if the (Silhouette Curve) option was selected when creating a 3D sketch. It is now possible using the newly added *Exclusion* area in the Create Silhouette Curve dialog box (as shown in Figure 2–6) that you can selectively exclude faces, straight faces, or internal faces from inclusion in the resulting curve.

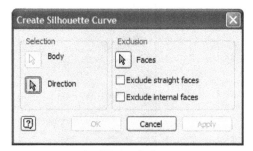

Figure 2–6

The modes shown in Figure 2–7 show examples of silhouette curves created on similar models.

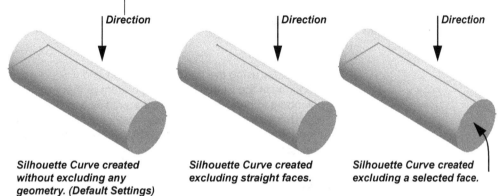

Silhouette Curve created without excluding any geometry. (Default Settings)

Silhouette Curve created excluding straight faces.

Silhouette Curve created excluding a selected face.

Figure 2–7

Curve on Face

As of Inventor 2017, it is now possible for a curve to be sketched directly on a face using the **Curve on Face** command. This enables you to easily locate the sketch directly on a non-planar face without having to project entities. To sketch a curve on a face, click (Curve on Face) in the Draw panel. You can select vertices, edges, or miscellaneous points to define the curve. The curve is placed on the face highlighted in red and is generated as a 3D interpolation spline, similar to that shown in Figure 2–8. Once sketched, you have access to the shortcut menu to close the sketch or add additional points. You can also use constraints and dimensions to fully define the curve.

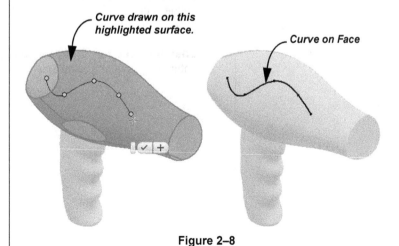

Curve drawn on this highlighted surface.

Curve on Face

Figure 2–8

Improving Sketch Accuracy

The following sketch enhancements were added in Inventor 2017 to improve accuracy while creating a 3D sketch. These options are all available in the Status Bar at the bottom of the 3D sketch and bring the tools in line with what is available for a 2D sketch.

- Consider using the ⬜ (Ortho Mode) and ⬜ (Snap Object) options in the Status Bar at the bottom of the graphics window to better control how the entities are sketched. With **Ortho Mode** enabled, you can restrict sketching to the X, Y, and Z planes. With **Snap Object** enabled, you can snap to existing entities when sketching new entities.

- Enable ⬜ (Dynamic Dimension) to ensure that the dynamic input toolbar displays when sketching to guarantee specific values. In a new sketch, this is toggled on by default. To clear its selection, you must disable it.

- Enable ⬜ (Infer Constraints) to ensure that constraints are automatically inferred while sketching. To toggle it off, disable this option.

Aligning and Reorienting the Sketch Triad

To accurately sketch entities in 3D, you can right-click and access commands that enable you to align and reorient the model. In addition to the **Align to Plane** option, the following shortcut menu options were added in 2017:

- **Orient Z** and **Orient to World:** Reorients the sketching triad to a custom Z direction or to the world coordinate system. To define a custom Z direction, you can select an edge, line, axis, plane, vertex or point.

- **Snap Intersection:** Snaps an entity to the intersection of entities. This is only available when **Ortho Mode** is enabled.

Modifying 3D Sketch Entities

The following enhancements have been added in Inventor 2017 for editing a 3D sketch:

- The Modify panel now has a new **3D Transform** option that enables you to reposition geometry in a 3D sketch. Once activated, you are provided with the transform triad and mini-toolbar. Select a manipulator handle on the triad to reposition the selected entity linearly, rotationally, or on a plane. The mini-toolbar updates as required and enables you to enter values to define the move. The mini-toolbar can also be used to control the orientation of the triad to the world, view, or local coordinate systems. In Figure 2–9, a spline entity is being moved along the X axis of the world coordinate system.

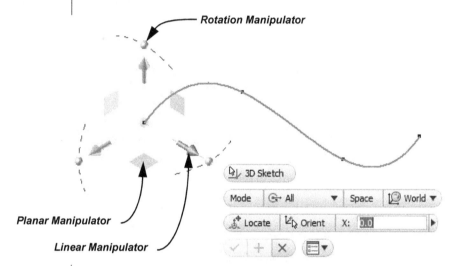

Figure 2–9

- You can now use standard copy and paste functionality to create copies of existing sketched entities in the same sketch or in different sketches. This enables you to efficiently duplicate entities in a 3D sketch. Use the 3D Transform tool to move the pasted entities, as required. If pasted in the same sketch the new entities are pasted over the source entities and must be moved.

- Prior to 2017, you could only drag a sketched entity by endpoints or centerpoints. Now, you can select anywhere on the entity to reposition it in a sketch.

Constraining 3D Sketched Entities

The available constraint options have been enhanced in Inventor 2017, as shown in Figure 2–10.

2016 Constrain Panel

2017 Constrain Panel

Figure 2–10

*Assigned constraints can be deleted by right-clicking on the constraint symbol in the graphics window and selecting **Delete** or by right-clicking and selecting **Delete** on the menu.*

- The **Coincident**, **Parallel**, **Tangent**, **Collinear**, **Perpendicular**, **Smooth (G2)**, **Fixed**, and **Equal** constraints can be used in the same way as in a 2D sketch. The **Equal** constraint was added to this list in 2017.

- The (On Face) constraint enables you to constrain points, lines, arc, or spline to a planar face. Optionally, you can constrain individual points to a curved face.

- The , , and constraint types can be used to constrain a line, curve, or spline handle to lie parallel with the X, Y, or Z axis, respectively.

- The , , and constraint types can be used to constrain a line, curve, or spline to lie parallel with the XY, YZ, or XZ axis, respectively.

Practice 2a

Creating a Curve on a Face

Practice Objective

- Create a curve on the existing face in a model.

In this practice, you will work in an existing model of a hairdryer that contains geometry for the main body and the handle. Using the new **Curve on Face** command, you will create a 3D sketched curve that will be used as the path for the swept cut shown in Figure 2–11.

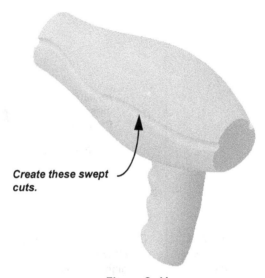

Create these swept cuts.

Figure 2–11

Task 1 - Create a curve on a surface of the hairdryer.

1. Launch Autodesk Inventor 2017, if not already running.

2. In the *Get Started* tab>Launch panel, select ⬚ (Projects). In the Projects dialog box, browse to the *C:\Autodesk Inventor 2017 Update Practice Files* folder. Select **2017 Update Practice Files.ipj** and click **Open**. The My Home dashboard enables you to set the active project if it has already been loaded, but cannot be used to locate and load a new project. This must be done in the Projects dialog box.

3. Open **Hairdryer.ipt** from the practice files folder. The main body and handle have been created for you. The next step is to add some detail to the main body.

4. In the *3D Model* tab>Sketch panel, click 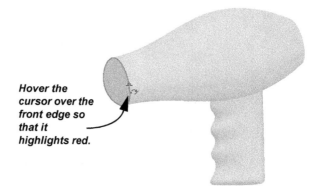 (Start 3D Sketch). The command can be found on the expanded **Start 2D Sketch** command.

5. In the *3D Sketch*>Draw panel, click (Curve on Face) to sketch a curve directly on a curved face.

6. Rotate the model similar to that shown in Figure 2–12.

7. Hover the cursor over the model so that the first point of the curve snaps to the front edge, as shown in Figure 2–12.

Hover the cursor over the front edge so that it highlights red.

Figure 2–12

You can select vertices, edges, or miscellaneous points to define the curve. The curve is placed on the face highlighted in red and is generated as a 3D interpolation spline.

8. Continue to place points on the face of the hairdryer, as shown in Figure 2–13. When placing the points, the red highlight reveals the face on which the spline points will be placed. In this model, ensure that all selections snap to the near face and not the back face. If they appear to snap to the back face, reposition the cursor before selecting.

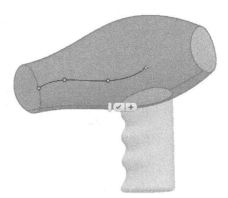

Figure 2–13

9. Continue to place additional spline points similar to that shown in Figure 2–14.

10. To complete the curve, ensure that the edge at the back of the hairdryer highlights red, which indicates that you are snapping to it.

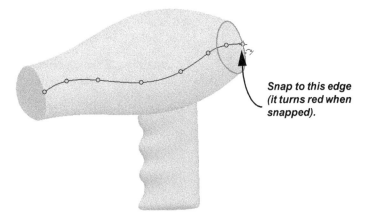

Snap to this edge (it turns red when snapped).

Figure 2–14

11. Right-click and select **Create** to complete the curve. The curve should display similar to that shown in Figure 2–15. Note that it may vary depending on your selection points.

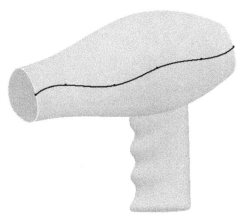

Figure 2–15

12. In the *3D Sketch*>Draw panel, click ✓ (Finish Sketch) or select **Finish 3D Sketch** in the context menu.

Prior to 2017, this curve would have had to been created using an intersection curve or projection onto a surface. This tool enabled you to easily sketch the required shape directly on the face.

Task 2 - Create a cut that sweeps along the curve.

In this task, you will create a 2D sketch to represent the profile of a cut that will be swept along the 3D curve that you just created.

1. Create a 2D sketch on the front planar face of the hairdryer, as shown in Figure 2–16.

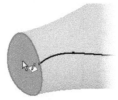

Figure 2–16

2. Project the endpoint of the curve and sketch a circular section located on the projected point, as shown in Figure 2–17. Enter **5** as the diameter of the circle.

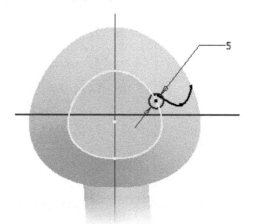

Figure 2–17

3. Complete the sketch.

4. Create a sweep that removes material from the model, as shown in Figure 2–18. The swept cut should remain parallel to the profile's sketch plane along the length of the cut.

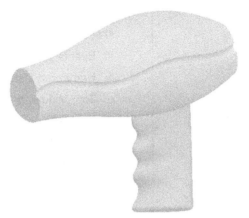

Figure 2–18

5. To complete the model, mirror the cut about the XY plane.

6. Save the model and close the window.

Chapter Review Questions

1. Which of the following are new formatting options that can be used in the Format Text dialog box when creating text in a sketch? (Select all that apply.)

   a. Bullets

   b. Numbered Lists

   c. Top, Middle, and Bottom Justification

   d. Colored Font

   e. Strike-Through Text

   f. Background Text Box Fill

2. Which of the following commands enables you to highlight planes in the graphics window to help identify a feature's sketch plane?

   a. **Visibility**

   b. **Share Sketch**

   c. **Properties**

   d. **Show Input**

3. When creating a Silhouette Curve in a 3D sketch, the *Exclusion* area enables you to independently select features that are to be excluded from the curve.

   a. True

   b. False

4. When you use the **Wrap to Surface** option while projecting a surface in a 3D sketch, you can only select a single entity to project onto at one time.

   a. True

   b. False

5. Which of the following four 3D sketch creation options enables you to use the Drawing tools and sketch 3D entities directly on a curved face?

   a. Intersection Curve

   b. Silhouette Curve

   c. Project to Surface

   d. Curve on Face

6. Which of the following best describes how the new Ortho Mode () tool can be used in a 3D sketch?

   a. It restricts sketching to the X, Y, and Z planes.

   b. It snaps to existing entities when sketching new entities.

   c. It enables the dynamic input toolbar for entering specific size values.

   d. It ensures that constraints are automatically inferred while sketching.

7. When manipulating a 3D sketch using the **3D Transform** command, which of the following can be done using the triad manipulator that displays on the sketch? (Select all that apply.)

   a. Rotate an entity by dragging it.

   b. Rotate an entity by entering values.

   c. Translate an entity by dragging it.

   d. Translate an entity by entering values.

   e. Change from the World to a Local Space.

   f. Control which transform handles displays on the model.

   g. Reposition the location of the triad manipulator.

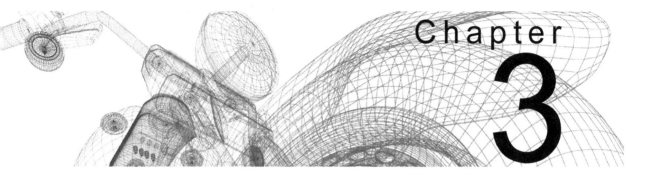

Chapter
3

Part Enhancements

In this chapter, you learn about the enhancements that have been introduced into the part modeling environment. These include improvements and new features in solid and surface modeling tools.

Learning Objectives in this Chapter

- Describe the enhancements used to improve the existing part modeling tools.
- Create a surface boundary patch that references a rail to refine the shape of the patch.
- Create ruled surface geometry.
- Describe the enhancements that improve the pattern and mirror tools.
- Use the new Relationships dialog box to identify the parent and child relationships between features.

3.1 Modeling Enhancements

Extrude

When creating extruded geometry in the Autodesk® Inventor® 2017software, you can now use the window selection technique to quickly select multiple closed sections that are to be extruded during the feature operation, as shown in Figure 3–1. Previously, you were able to select multiple sections; however, selection was required to be done manually.

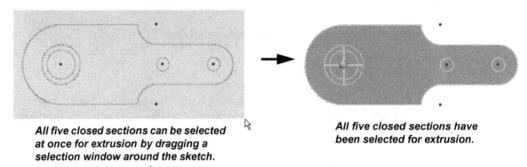

All five closed sections can be selected at once for extrusion by dragging a selection window around the sketch.

All five closed sections have been selected for extrusion.

Figure 3–1

Parting Line Drafts

The following Parting Line Draft enhancements have been added to the 2016 version of the software.

Parting Tool

Surfaces can now be selected as the parting tool when a Parting Line Draft is created, as shown in Figure 3–2. This provides an alternative to creating a 3D sketch to define the parting line.

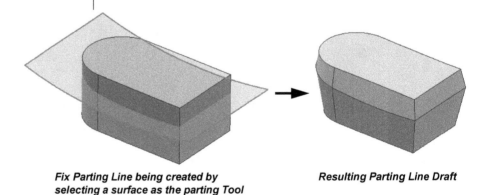

Fix Parting Line being created by selecting a surface as the parting Tool

Resulting Parting Line Draft

Figure 3–2

Move Parting Line

When creating a Parting Line Draft, you now have options to create it as  (Fix Parting Line) or (Move Parting Line) Draft. By default, the Parting Line draft is created using the Fixed Parting Line ( ) option, which ensures that the geometry remains the same size at the parting line and that draft is added above or below. Alternatively, the new ( ) Move Parting Line option can be selected to add material at the parting line. When the **Move Parting Line** option is selected, the Face Draft dialog box updates, as shown in Figure 3–3.

Figure 3–3

Figure 3–4 shows an example of how a curve was used as the parting line and the resulting drafts when both the (Fix Parting Line) and (Move Parting Line) options are used. In the Move Parting Line example, note how the material was added at the parting line to ensure that the overall geometry remained the same size.

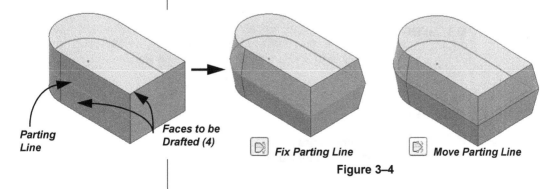

Parting Line   *Faces to be Drafted (4)*   *Fix Parting Line*   *Move Parting Line*

Figure 3–4

When using the 🖻 (Move Parting Line) option, you can customize the draft by setting static edges on the draft geometry and specifying how the draft value is added.

- To set static edges, enable 🖎 (Fixed Edges) once draft faces have been selected and select the individual edges that will not change. Alternatively, click 🖻 (Select Boundary) to select multiple edges automatically.

- To clear all selected fixed edges, click 🖼 (Clear All). The selection of fixed edges can only be customized in the Face Draft dialog box.

- To specify how the draft value is added, select the options shown in Figure 3–5. The draft angle can be specified so that it is on both sides using 🖻 (Angle for Both), 🖻 (Angle for Top), or 🖻 (Angle for Bottom).

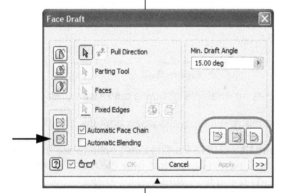 

Figure 3–5

iFeatures

When adding an iFeature prior to 2017, it could only be set to affect (i.e. cut) one single solid body with the operation. It is now possible to select multiple bodies when working in a multi-body design.

Make Part/Make Component

When creating a part or component from a multi-body or sketch blocks, it is now possible to access the **Make Part** and **Make Components** command on the right-click Context menu. This enhancement was introduced in Inventor 2017 (R2).

Replace Face

The **Replace Face** command has been expanded to enable the selection of a solid when selecting the *New Face* reference. Previously, you were only able to select a surface, quilt, or workplane.

Boundary Patch

The following enhancements have been added to Autodesk Inventor when using the **Patch** command to create a boundary patch surface.

- As of 2016, Boundary patch geometry can be created without having to select a fully closed loop(s). To create the patch, clear the **Automatic Edge Chain** option and select each required edge reference. As you select edges, a preview displays (whenever possible), as shown in Figure 3–6.

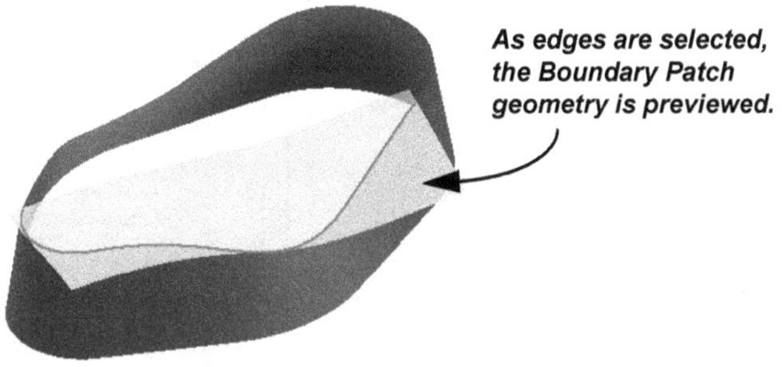

If the selection set does not preview a surface, the geometry cannot be created. As edges are added to the selection, set the preview and size of the surface update to incorporate the new edge.

As edges are selected, the Boundary Patch geometry is previewed.

Figure 3–6

- To further refine the shape of the patch surface, it is now possible to assign guide rails. This functionality was introduced in Inventor 2017 and provides you with added flexibility in creating complex shapes. To use guide rails in a Boundary Patch, click ⌖ (Guide Rails) and select curves or points to drive the shape of the patch, as shown in Figure 3–7.

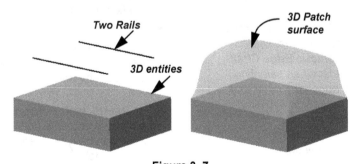

Two Rails

3D Patch surface

3D entities

Figure 3–7

Ruled Surfaces

The new **Ruled Surface** option enables you to create normal, tangent, and swept surfaces. A ruled surface is a surface where a straight line lies at every point on the surface. Common uses for this type of surface includes creating parting surfaces for mold design, creating surfaces that can split a body, or adding pockets.

How To: Create a Ruled Surface

1. Click (Ruled Surface) to open the Ruled Surface dialog box, as shown in Figure 3–8.

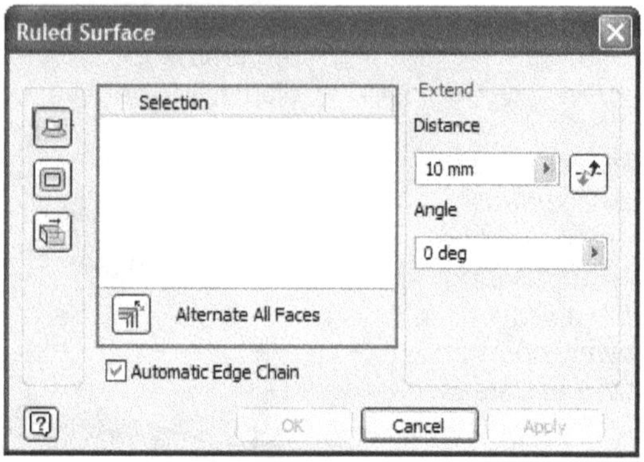

Figure 3–8

2. On the left-hand side of the dialog box, select the type of ruled surface.

The dialog box options vary depending on the type of ruled surface you select.

- Click (Normal) to create a ruled surface that remains normal along the edge reference.
- Click (Tangent) to create a ruled surface that remains tangent along the edge reference.
- Click (Sweep) to create a ruled surface that follows a direction vector along the edge reference.

3. Define references to create the ruled surface.

*For Tangent and Normal ruled surfaces, select **Automatic Edge Chain** so that when selecting an edge, any edge that is tangent to it is also selected. Clear this option to select individual edges.*

- For Tangent or Normal ruled surfaces, select an edge reference to create the surface. Multiple edges can be selected. The references are listed in the *Edges Selection* area.
- For Sweep ruled surfaces, select a sketch to define the path and a vector to define the direction. The direction vector can be a face, edge, or axis. The sketch must exist in the model.

4. Enter a value in the *Distance* field to extend the edge(s) or sketch.

- Select 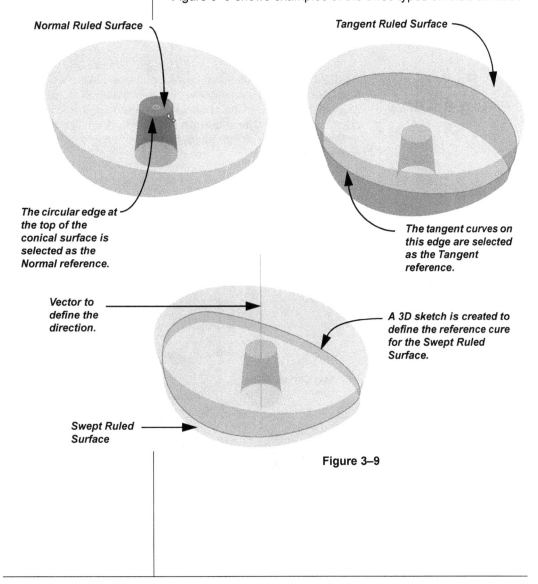 (Flip) to reverse the extension direction.

- Select (Alternate All Faces) to reverse the faces that are being used to define the directions.

5. (Optional) Enter an *Angle* value for the ruled surface.
6. Click **OK** to complete the ruled surface.

Figure 3–9 shows examples of the three types of ruled surfaces.

Normal Ruled Surface

Tangent Ruled Surface

The circular edge at the top of the conical surface is selected as the Normal reference.

The tangent curves on this edge are selected as the Tangent reference.

Vector to define the direction.

A 3D sketch is created to define the reference cure for the Swept Ruled Surface.

Swept Ruled Surface

Figure 3–9

3.2 Duplication Tools

The following enhancements now provide additional flexibility when patterning and mirroring geometry.

Duplicating Multiple Solid Bodies

As of 2016, when patterning or mirroring a solid body, you can now select multiple solid bodies when using either the **Join** ( ) or **Create new bodies** ( ) patterning options. The **Solid** reference selection option is no longer optimized for a single selection and you can hold <Ctrl> to select multiple bodies for patterning.

Patterning Along a Curve

As of 2016, solid bodies can now be patterned along a curve, as has been previously possible with feature patterns. To pattern along a curve, select the bodies to be patterned, the reference curve, and select **Curve Length** in the drop-down list, as shown in Figure 3–10. Complete the pattern by entering a count value and selecting **OK**.

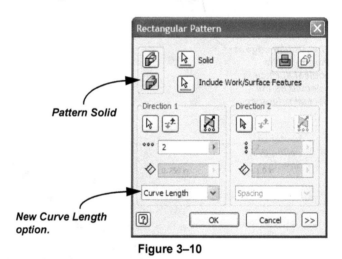

Figure 3–10

Circular Pattern Orientation

An *Orientation* area in the Circular Pattern dialog box has been added in Inventor 2017, which enables you to orient the patterned instances in the model.

- Select (Rotational) to ensure that the patterned feature's orientation is rotated, as it extends through the pattern angle.

- Select (Fixed) to ensure that the patterned feature's orientation remains the same as the original feature, as it extends through the pattern angle. When defining a **Fixed** orientation, you can change the default Base Point, if required.

Figure 3–11 shows examples of both orientation options that are available.

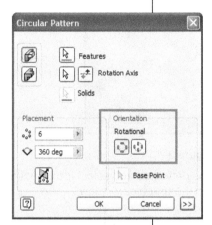

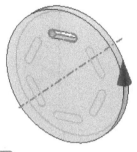

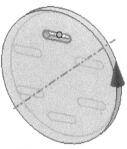

Rotational Orientation   Fixed Orientation

Figure 3–11

Sketched Driven Patterns

You can create multiple copies of parts or features on a part by creating a pattern. Examples of a pattern of slots are shown in Figure 3–12.

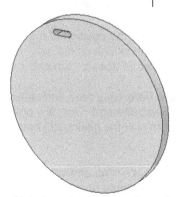

Slot-shaped cut to be patterned on the face of the cylinder.

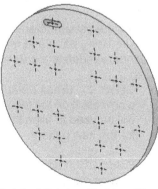

Sketched Points added to a 2D sketch to define pattern placement.

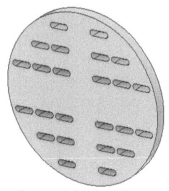

Patterned slot-shaped cuts.

Figure 3–12

How To: Create a Sketched Driven Pattern

1. In the *3D Model* tab>Pattern panel, click  (Sketch Driven Pattern). The Sketch Driven Pattern dialog box opens as shown in Figure 3–13.

Figure 3–13

2. Select the object type to be patterned and select the object(s) in the Model Browser or in the graphics window.

   - Select [icon] to pattern individual features.

   - Select [icon] to pattern a solid.

3. Select an existing sketch to define the placement of the pattern.
   - The sketch can be 2D or 3D and must contain sketch points. The sketch points will define the placement of the pattern feature.

4. Define the pattern reference. To refine the position of the feature being patterned relative to the sketch points, you can optionally redefine the Base Point and Faces for the pattern.

   - Select [icon] (Base Point) in the *Reference* area and select a new point on the feature being patterned. This new point will be used to align the feature with the sketched points for the new pattern.

   - Select [icon] (Faces) in the *Reference* area and select a face on the model to set the occurrence orientation. This reference defines the normal direction for the pattern.

5. (Optional) Refine how the feature pattern is generated using the *Creation Method* area (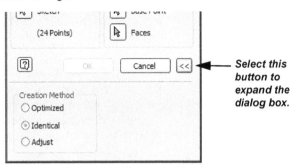). The expanded dialog box is shown in Figure 3–14.

Figure 3–14

- The *Creation Method* area contains options to control how the pattered geometry is calculated. The three options are the same as those in the *Compute* area for rectangular patterns. Refer to their description in the *Rectangular pattern* topic for more information.

6. Click **OK** to complete the pattern. Alternatively, you can right-click and select **OK (Enter)**.

3.3 General Design Tools

Measure

As of 2016, you can now measure an angle to the midpoint of any segment by hovering the cursor over the midpoint of a segment until a yellow dot displays.

Direct Edit

As of 2016, there is now a new **Scale** command that has been added to the Direct Edit tool. This enables you to scale the geometry uniformly using the options shown on the left in Figure 3–15 or scale the body geometry non-uniformly using the options shown on the right in Figure 3–15

Figure 3–15

Feature Relationships

For a better overview of the relationships between features, you can now right-click on a feature name in the Model Browser and select **Relationships**. The Relationships dialog box opens similar to that shown in Figure 3–16. This reveals the relationships between features and enables you to make changes, if required. This functionality was added to the Model Browser in 2017.

To select features directly in the Graphics Window, ensure that **Select Features** is the active option in the selection filter list.

The Parents area lists all parent features of the selected feature.

The currently selected feature is listed here.

The Children area lists all child features of the selected feature.

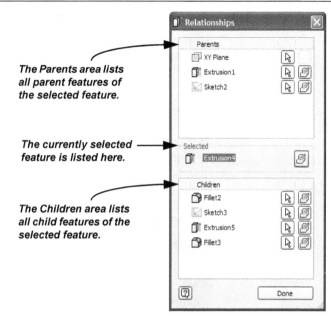

Figure 3–16

- **(Make Selected):** Enables you to set any of the parent or child features as the new selected item.

- **(Edit Feature):** Enables you to access the Edit Feature dialog box for any of the parent or child features.

Practice 3a | Ruled Surface Creation

Practice Objective

- Create normal, tangent, and swept ruled surfaces.

In this practice, you will learn how to use the **Ruled Surface** command to create normal, tangent, and swept ruled surfaces to complete a model. Finally, you will use the **Stitch** and **Thicken** commands to create solid geometry from surface geometry. The completed geometry is shown (in a top and bottom view) in Figure 3–17.

Figure 3–17

Task 1 - Create a ruled surface using the Normal type.

1. Open **Ruled_Surface.ipt** from the practice files folder.

2. In the *3D Model* tab>Surface panel, click (Ruled Surface). The Ruled Surface dialog box opens, as shown in Figure 3–18.

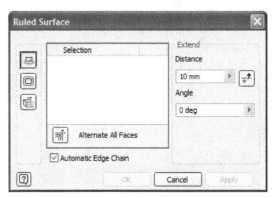

Figure 3–18

*The **Shaded with Edges** Visual Style setting was assigned to improve the clarity of the images.*

3. In the Ruled Surface dialog box, ensure that 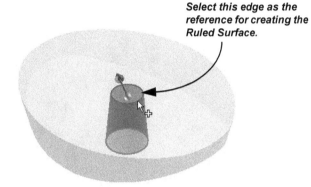 (Normal) is selected, if not already set.

4. Select the circular edge, as shown in Figure 3–19.

5. Set the *Distance* to **10 mm**, if not already set as the default value. The surface previewed should be pointing toward the center of the selected circle, as shown in Figure 3–19. If not, flip the orientation using the button.

Select this edge as the reference for creating the Ruled Surface.

Figure 3–19

6. Click **Apply** to create the surface and leave the dialog box open to create additional surfaces.

7. In the Top view, zoom in on the surface. Note that the new ruled surface is perpendicular to the conical surface that is adjacent to it, not parallel to the bottom of the model. Figure 3–20 shows a sectioned view through the XY plane to visualize the ruled surface.

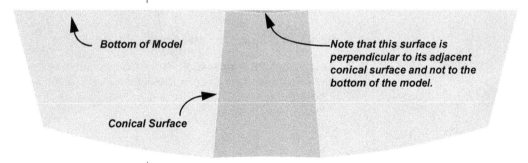

Bottom of Model

Note that this surface is perpendicular to its adjacent conical surface and not to the bottom of the model.

Conical Surface

Figure 3–20

Task 2 - Create a ruled surface using the Tangent type.

1. With the **Ruled Surface** command still active, in the Rule Surface dialog box, select ▣ (Tangent).

2. Set the *Distance* to **25 mm** and ensure that the **Automatic Edge Chain** option is selected.

3. Select the edge shown in Figure 3–21.

4. The preview of the tangent ruled surface displays as shown in Figure 3–21. Click **Apply** to create the surface. Leave the dialog box open to create additional surfaces.

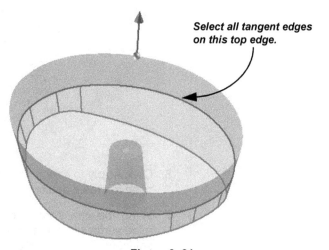

Select all tangent edges on this top edge.

Figure 3–21

Task 3 - Create a ruled surface using the Sweep type.

1. Select ▣ (Sweep) to create a swept ruled surface.

2. Ensure that the **Automatic Edge Chain** option is selected and select the lower edge of the outer surface, as shown in Figure 3–22.

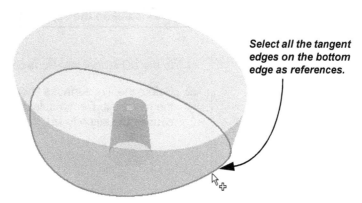

Select all the tangent edges on the bottom edge as references.

Figure 3–22

3. Select (Vector), if not already active. Expand the **Origin** node and select the **Z Axis** as the sweep direction vector.

4. Set the *Distance* to **5 mm** and flip the surface creation direction, if required. A preview of the swept ruled surface displays as shown in Figure 3–23.

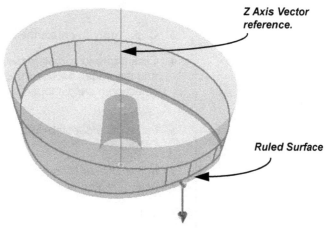

Z Axis Vector reference.

Ruled Surface

Figure 3–23

5. Click **OK** to create the surface.

Task 4 - Thicken the surfaces to create a solid part.

1. In the *3D Model* tab>Surface panel, click 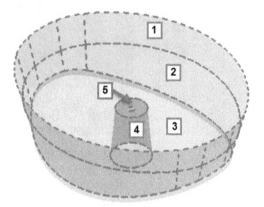 (Stitch).

2. Select the five surfaces shown in Figure 3–24 to add them to the new quilt. Do not select the swept ruled surface, as this causes the stitch to fail.

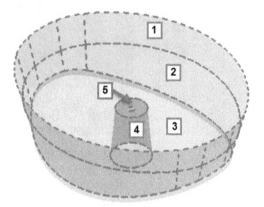

Figure 3–24

3. Click **Apply** to create the stitched surface quilt.

4. Click **Done** to complete the command. The surface updates and the edges between the tangent ruled surface and its selection have disappeared.

5. In the *3D Model* tab>Modify panel, click (Thicken/ Offset).

6. In the Thicken/Offset dialog box, select **Quilt** and select the newly created quilt.

7. Set the *Distance* to **2.5 mm**.

8. Flip the thicken direction, if required, so that the material is created to the inside of the part.

9. Click **OK** to thicken the part and create a new solid body.

10. Start the Thicken/Offset command again. Ensure that the

    ⊟ (Join) and **Quilt** selections are active and the *Distance* value remains at **2.5 mm**.

11. Select the swept ruled surface quilt. Flip the direction to create the solid geometry to the inside of the surface, if required.

12. Click **OK** to thicken the quilt and complete the command.

13. In the *View* tab>Visibility panel, expand the Object Visibility drop-down list and clear the **Construction Surfaces** selection.

    Figure 3–25 shows the completed model from the top and bottom.

Figure 3–25

14. Save and close the part.

Practice 3b | Boundary Patch

Practice Objective

- Create a Boundary Patch using a rail.

In this practice, you will create a boundary patch and use the new **Rail** option available in this tool, which enables you to refine the shape of the patch by having it reference another entity (Rail). The completed solid geometry that you will create is shown in Figure 3–26.

Figure 3–26

Task 1 - Create a Boundary Patch to fill a hole in the geometry.

1. Open **Boundary_Patch.ipt** from the practice files folder. Note that in the Model Browser, a number of features already exist. This surface was initially imported from another CAD system, stitched, and faces were deleted.

2. In the *3D Model* tab>Surface panel, click ⬚ (Patch).

3. Select **Automatic Edge Chain**, if it is not already selected. This enables you to select all the adjacent edges together instead of selecting them individually.

4. Select the circular edges bounding the face area shown in Figure 3–27. A flat face immediately previews on the model.

*As of 2016, with the **Automatic Edge Chain** option disabled, a preview of the boundary patch displays and updates as you select each edge. If it doesn't preview, it can't be created.*

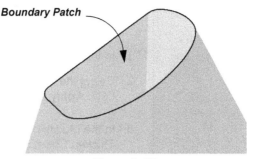

Figure 3–27

5. In the Boundary Patch dialog box, in the *Condition* area, in the selected edge drop-down list, click 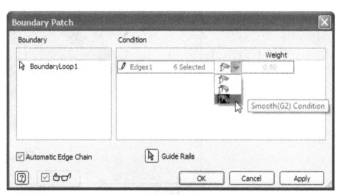 (Smooth G2), as shown in Figure 3–28, for the edges that define the patch. This creates a smooth continuous condition between the patch and adjacent faces on the selected edge.

Figure 3–28

6. Maintain the default *Weight* value of **0.5**. Click **OK**. The model displays as shown in Figure 3–29.

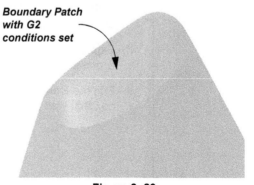

Figure 3–29

Task 2 - Stitch surfaces and create a solid.

1. In the *3D Model* tab>Surface panel, click ⊞ (Stitch).

2. Select the new surface and the existing stitched surface. Click **Apply** and **Done**.

3. In the Modify panel, click ⬦ (Thicken/Offset). The Thicken/Offset dialog box opens.

4. Select **Quilt** to easily select the stitched surface.

5. Select the stitched surface and set the *Distance* to **4 mm**.

6. Click **OK**. The solid geometry is created with a **4 mm** thickness, as shown in Figure 3–30.

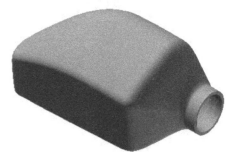

Figure 3–30

Task 3 - Modify the boundary patch to manipulate the geometry at the end of the bottle.

1. In the Model Browser, toggle on the visibility of the **Rail Sketch** sketch. This is a simple linear entity that was added to the design and will be used to change the shape of the boundary patch.

2. Expand the last **Stitch Surface** feature listed in the Model Browser. It has consumed the **Boundary Patch** feature.

3. Edit the **Boundary Patch** feature to open the original dialog box that was used to create it.

4. Click  (Guide Rails) and select the linear entity that was created in the Rail Sketch sketch. The preview updates to show how the new rail reference has changed the geometry.

5. Click **OK**. Note how the shape at the end of the bottle has changed, as shown in Figure 3–31.

Figure 3–31

6. Save the model and close the window.

Practice 3c | Sketched Driven Pattern

Practice Objective

- Create a sketched driven pattern.

In this practice, you will learn how to use the new **Sketch Driven** command to create a pattern that follows a sketch. The completed geometry is shown in Figure 3–32.

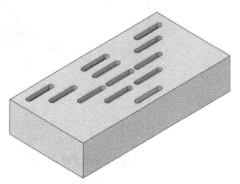

Figure 3–32

Task 1 - Open a model and create slotted cut that will be patterned.

1. Open **Housing.ipt** from the practice files folder. The model displays as shown in Figure 3–33.

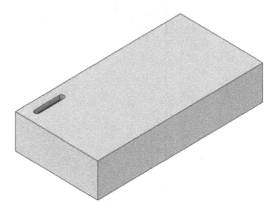

Figure 3–33

Task 2 - Create the sketch to drive the pattern.

1. Create a new sketch on the top face of the model. Project the XY plane (to assign symmetry), sketch construction lines, and add sketch points similar to that shown in Figure 3–34. For this practice, dimensions are not required as you are just learning to create a pattern. To parametrically place patterned instances, the sketch should be fully dimensioned and constrained. Note that each sketch point will become a reference point for placing a patterned instance.

A sketch that is being used for a sketch driven pattern can be 2D or 3D and must contain sketch points. The sketch points will define the placement of the pattern feature.

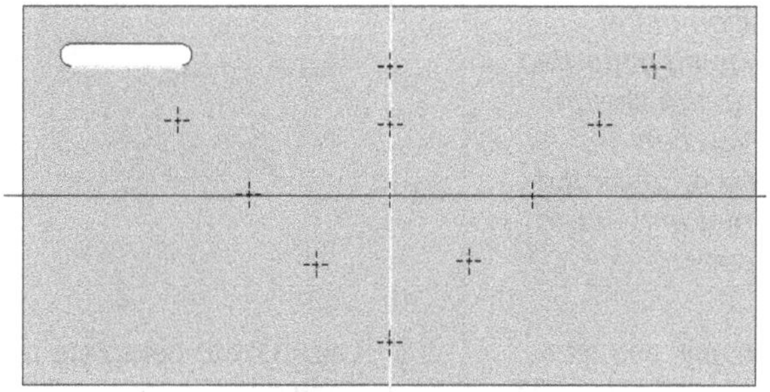

Figure 3–34

2. Complete the sketch.

Task 3 - Create the sketch driven pattern.

1. In the *3D Model* tab>Pattern panel, click ⛁ (Sketch Driven Pattern). The Sketch Driven Pattern dialog box opens as shown in Figure 3–35. Note that 11 points are immediately selected as placement references. This is because the points all exist in the sketch that was created.

Figure 3–35

If multiple sketches existed in the model prior to pattern creation you would be required to select a sketch.

By default, the Base Point and Faces references are preselected. To refine the position of the feature being patterned relative to the sketch points, you can optionally redefine the Base Point and Faces for the pattern.

Alternatively, you can right-click and select OK (Enter).

2. Select 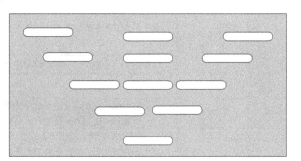 (Pattern individual features) and select the slotted cut in the graphics window. The pattern previews in the graphics window, as shown in Figure 3–36.

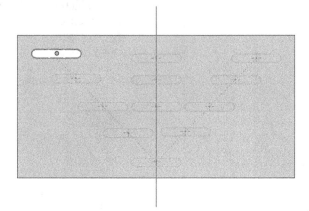

Figure 3–36

3. Click **OK** to complete the pattern. The pattern displays as shown in Figure 3–37.

Figure 3–37

Task 4 - Redefine the sketch to modify the pattern.

1. Expand the **Sketch Driven Pattern** node in the Model Browser and double-click the sketch to edit it.

2. Add additional points to the sketch so that the pattern updates similar to that shown in Figure 3–38.

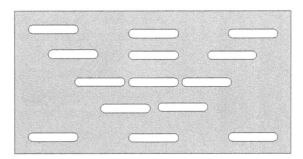

Figure 3–38

3. Save the model and close the window.

Chapter Review Questions

1. Which of the following statements about Parting Line Draft is true? (Select all that apply.)

   a. A surface can be selected as the *Parting Tool* reference.

   b. Material can be added to the model along the parting line.

   c. When creating a Fixed Parting Line Draft, you can select edges to remain fixed while creating the draft.

   d. Additional options are available when creating a Move Parting Line Draft to define how the angle is measured.

2. When replacing a face, which of the following entity types can be selected as the new reference? (Select all that apply.)

   a. Surface

   b. Quilt

   c. Workplane

   d. Solid

3. Similar to a Loft feature, guide rails can be used to create a surface using the **Patch** option.

   a. True

   b. False

4. Which of the following new Ruled Surface features enable you to select a reference surface and create a new surface? (Select all that apply.)

   a. Extrude

   b. Normal

   c. Tangent

   d. Sweep

5. When using the **Rectangular Pattern** option in a multi-solid model, multiple bodies can be patterned at the same time if they are being joined (⊟); however, if they are being created as individual bodies (⬚), they must be patterned individually.

   a. True

   b. False

6. Which of the following options in the Circular Pattern dialog box enables you to set the orientation of the resulting patterned instances?

   a. [icon]

   b. [icon]

   c. [icon]

   d. [icon]

7. When creating a sketched driven pattern, the Sketch Driven Pattern dialog box provides options for placing the sketched points required to generate the pattern.

   a. True

   b. False

8. Which of the following statements about the Relationships dialog box shown in Figure 3–39 are true? (Select all that apply.)

Figure 3–39

   a. All parent and child relationships for **Extrusion1** are listed.

   b. The [icon] option can be used to edit any feature or sketch in the dialog box.

   c. **Sketch 5** was used to create **Extrusion5**.

   d. **Extrusion2** is a parent of **Extrusion1**.

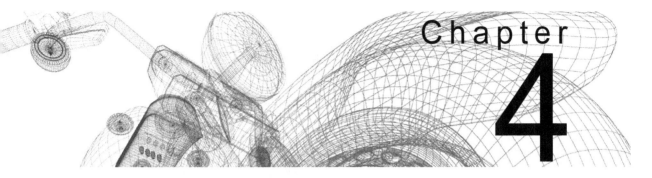

Assembly Enhancements

In this chapter, you learn about the changes that have been introduced in the Autodesk® Inventor® software that improve the process of working with assembly files. The enhancements discussed will include changes to the interface and how you interact with an assembly to investigate constraint failure, cross-part references, and analyze for interference. You will also learn how to set a component to a transparent display style, pattern about a mid-plane, and replace multiple components in an assembly at one time.

Learning Objective in this Chapter

*   Describe the general enhancements that affect the assembly tools available in the software.

4.1 General Enhancements

Assemble Tab

The following changes have been made to the *Assemble* tab in the 2016 release of the software:

- By default, the **Bill of Materials** and **Parameters** options are now included on the new Manage panel, as shown in Figure 4–1.

- While the **Copy** command was previously available in the compressed list of options, it has now been moved in the Pattern panel, as shown in Figure 4–1.

Figure 4–1

Transparent Components

The **Transparent** command added in 2017 enables you to set the visibility of an assembly component as transparent. Once set, the component cannot be selected but it remains visible in a transparent display style, as shown in Figure 4–2.

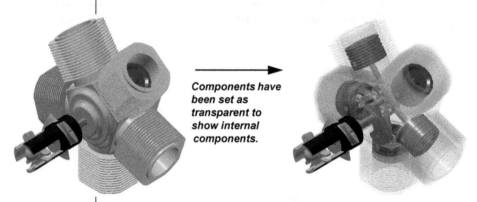

Components have been set as transparent to show internal components.

Figure 4–2

*Alternatively, in the component's iProperties dialog box, on the Occurrence tab, select **Transparent**.*

- To set a component to transparent, right-click on the component name in the Model Browser or in the graphics window and select **Transparent**.

- To undo the **Transparent** command, reselect the component and clear the option.

Sick Constraints

Prior to 2016, when assembly constraints failed and the Design Doctor was presented, you had to deal with each constraint individually. It is now possible to remove or suppress multiple failed constraints at the same time. You can do this by selecting all of the constraints using <Shift> or <Ctrl> (as shown in Figure 4–3) and then use the **Delete** or **Suppress** treatment options on all of them at once.

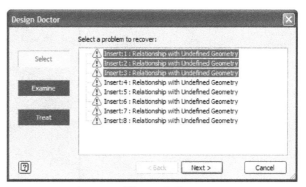

Figure 4–3

Assembly Patterns

An odd number count should be entered to create the pattern evenly on both sides.

As of 2016, when patterning assembly components, a Midplane option ( ) is now available (shown in Figure 4–4) to create the pattern so that it is distributed on both sides of the original component.

Figure 4–4

Mirror Components

The **Mirror Components** command in the assembly environment has been enhanced in 2017 (R2) to provide new functionality when duplicating components in an assembly. The new interface is shown in Figure 4–5 and is described below.

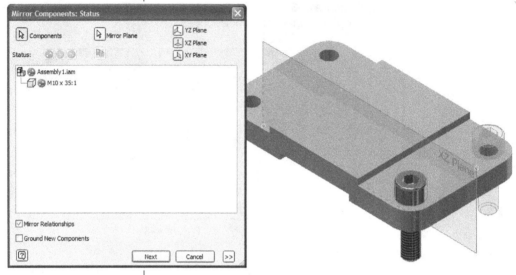

Figure 4–5

- Use the new plane icons (⬜, ⬜, or ⬜) to set the plane in which the component will be mirrored. This provides an alternative to displaying the origin planes or selecting the mirror plane from the Model Browser.

- Enable **Mirror Relationships** to apply the constraints and joints once the component is mirrored.

- Enable **Ground New Components** to automatically ground the new mirrored components.

Copy Components

Similar to the Mirror Components dialog box, the Copy Components dialog box has new **Copy Relationships** and **Ground New Components** options similar to those used to mirror.

Bill of Materials

Prior to Inventor 2017 (R2), the Bill of Materials dialog box could be used to open files; however, you could only open one component at a time. It is now possible to select multiple components and open them all at once, as shown in Figure 4–6.

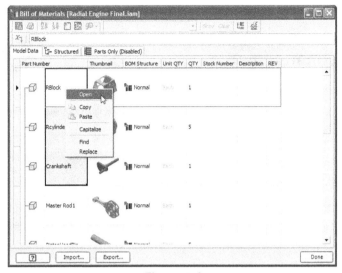

Figure 4–6

Interference Analysis

The following two enhancements have been introduced in 2016 to ease the use of the interference analysis tool:

- Components can now be added to the selection set using the crossing-window selection tool. This can be used as an alternative to selecting components individually in the Model Browser or graphics window.

- If interference is detected, you can zoom to the interference in the model by double-clicking on the entry or clicking $\mathcal{P}$ in the Interference Detected dialog box as shown in Figure 4–7.

Double-click on the interference item to zoom to it in the model or click $\mathcal{P}$.

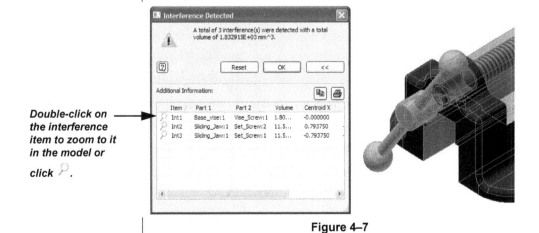

Figure 4–7

Cross-Part Reference Enhancements

Enhancements in the Inventor 2017 Model Browser now make cross-part references in an assembly easier to identify.

- The component name used in creating the reference is now identified in the browser node, as shown in Figure 4–8.

- Parent geometry can be opened from the Model Browser by right-clicking and select **Open References**, as shown in Figure 4–8.

- Unique Icons (as shown in Figure 4–8) are now associated with the reference to help identify the source. The entity types include: edge ( ), loop ( ), face ( ), sketch geometry ( ) and DWG geometry ( ).

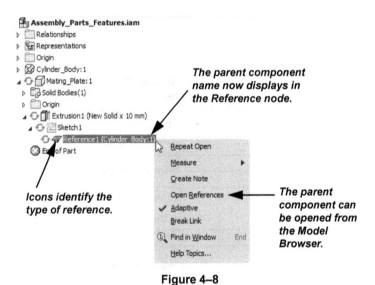

Figure 4–8

Replacing Components

As of 2016, the **Replace** command now supports the multi-selection of components, as shown in Figure 4–9. Previously, in order to replace some, but not all instances, you had to replace them individually. This enhancement provides a much faster method for the replacement of components.

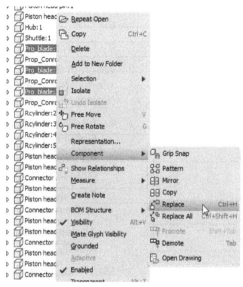

Figure 4–9

Graphics Performance

As of 2016, a new Application Option (**Disable Automatic Refinement**) has been added to the *Display* tab, as shown in Figure 4–10. This option enables you to control the faceting in both large assemblies and complex model geometry. Disabling automatic refinement provides a coarser model display and improves graphics performance. Coarse faceting is used until you select the **Refine Appearance** command in the *View* tab.

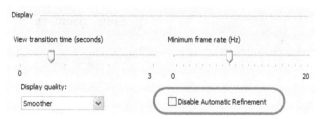

Figure 4–10

Chapter Review Questions

1. When a component is set to **Transparent** in a large assembly, only the component's visibility is affected, you can still select the component in the Model Browser.

   a. True

   b. False

2. Which of the following statements about conducting an interference analysis in Autodesk Inventor 2017 are true?. (Select all that apply.)

   a. All components being analyzed must be explicitly selected in the Model Browser.

   b. An interference analysis can be conducted on all components in the assembly at once.

   c. To review a detected interference, you can double-click it in the results list.

   d. All detected interferences are highlighted in red on the model.

3. Match the icons with the reference type that they identify in the Model Browser when a cross-part reference is created in an assembly model.

   a. Edge   _____

   b. Loop   _____

   c. Face   _____

   d. Sketch geometry   _____

   e. DWG geometry   _____

4. The Midplane option () available in the Pattern dialog box enables you to create the pattern so that it is distributed on both sides of a selected reference plane.

   a. True

   b. False

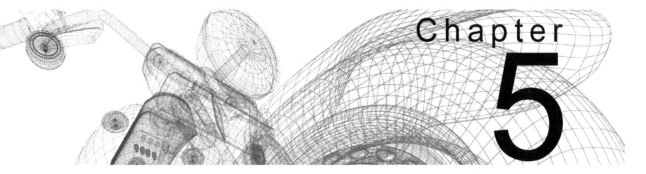

Chapter

5

Presentation Files

The presentation tools available in the Autodesk® Inventor® 2017 software enable you to create Snapshot views and animations to help document an assembly. A presentation file can be used to indicate how parts relate to each other and create an exploded view for a drawing. Animating the exploded view of the assembly enables you to further show how components fit together in the assembly. With the release of Autodesk Inventor 2017 software, the interface for this tool has been completely redesigned.

Learning Objectives in this Chapter

- Understand how presentation files can be used to document an assembly model.
- Create a presentation file with an animation of how an assembly is to be assembled.
- Create a presentation file with Snapshot views that can be used in drawing views.
- Publish a presentation file to create images and videos.

5.1 Creating Presentations

To create an exploded view of an assembly, you must use a presentation file. In a presentation file, you can move or rotate the components relative to one another and add trails to indicate how they relate in the assembly. This can be stored as an animation or as static images. An exploded view of an assembly is shown in Figure 5–1.

If a component dimension is modified or if a component is removed or added in the assembly, the presentation file updates to incorporate the changes.

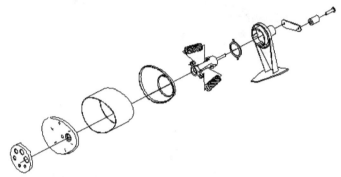

Figure 5–1

The first step in creating a presentation file is to start a new file based on a Presentation template (.IPN). To access the presentation templates, you can use any of the following:

- Click ⬜ (New) in the Launch panel, the Quick Access toolbar, or in the **File** menu. Select an *.IPN template in the Create New File dialog box and click **Create**. You might need to scroll down in the list to locate this template.

To verify the default presentation template in the My Home tab, click

⚙ *(Configure Default Templates) and review the settings in the Configure Default Template dialog box.*

- Click 🔧 (Presentation) in the *My Home* tab to create a new file with the default template.

- In an open assembly model, right-click on the assembly name at the top of the Model Browser and select **Create Presentation**. Once selected, you will be prompted for the template to be used.

Once the presentation file is created, the Presentation environment displays and you are immediately prompted to select a model for the first scene. Using the Insert dialog box, you can navigate to and open the model that will be used in the presentation. The *Presentation* tab becomes the active tab and the interface includes a Model Browser, Snapshot Views browser, and the Storyboard panel, as shown in Figure 5–2.

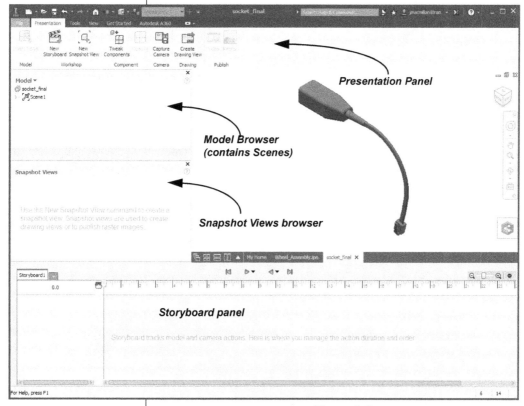

Figure 5–2

A presentation file is automatically created with an initial scene called **Scene1**.

- A file can consist of multiple scenes, all of which are independent and can reference different source models. To create additional scenes, right-click at the top of the Model Browser and select **Create Scene**.

- The model inserted in the last scene is listed at the top of the Model Browser; however, each scene contains the model that was initially assigned to it.

- Each scene can contain Snapshot views and storyboards.

Hint: Inserting Models

When selecting the model to be inserted into a scene, you can click **Options** to open the File Open Options dialog box, which enables you to:

- Insert an associative or non-associative version of a Design View Representation. If the **Associative** option is disabled on insertion, any changes in the selected Design View Representation will not update in the presentation file.

- Insert a specific Positional Representation of the model.

- Insert a specific Level of Detail Representation of the model.

If the representation of the model needs to be changed after it has been added to the scene, right-click the **Scene** node in the Model Browser and select **Representations**. You will be presented with the same File Open Options dialog box and can change the representation that is used.

5.2 Storyboards

The Storyboard panel at the bottom of the graphics window contains the list of storyboards that exist in a Presentation file. Each storyboard is included on its own tab. A storyboard can be used for the following:

Snapshot views can be created at specific points along the timeline. This is discussed further in the next topic.

- Creating an animation of the model that records component movements (i.e., assembly/disassembly).

- Creating actions to represent changes in component visibility and opacity at specific times in an animation.

- Capturing changes in camera position at specific times in an animation.

Figure 5–3 shows the components of the Storyboard panel used to create and play animations.

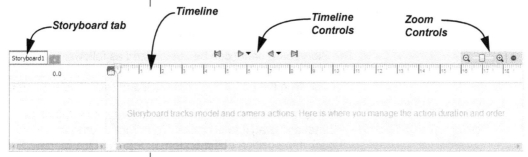

Figure 5–3

When a presentation file is created, a single storyboard is included. Additional storyboards can be included, as required. Storyboards can be independent of one another or they can work in combination with one another.

How To: Create a Storyboard

1. Activate the scene to which the storyboard will be added by double-clicking the scene name in the Model Browser.

2. In the Presentation tab>Workshop panel, click (New Storyboard). Alternatively, in the Storyboard panel at the bottom of the graphics window, click adjacent to the Storyboard tabs.

3. Select the *Storyboard Type* in the New Storyboard dialog box, as shown in Figure 5–4.

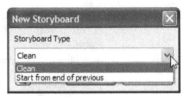

Figure 5–4

- **Clean:** Creates a new storyboard that uses the default appearance and camera settings for the active scene.
- **Start From End of Previous:** Creates a new storyboard that is started from the end of another storyboard. The component positions, visibility, opacity, and camera settings from the previous storyboard is used as the starting point for the new one.

4. Click **OK**.

Hint: Storyboard Panel Customization

The Storyboard panel can be customized as follows:

- Click ● in the panel to compress it and click ● to expand it.

- Select and hold the left mouse button at the far left of the panel and drag it to undock it. To redock it, drag its titlebar back into position at the bottom of the graphics window.

- Use ⊖ ☐ ⊕ to zoom in or out on the timeline's scale.

Animations

An animation consists of movements that are applied to selected components in the assembly. The movements are called *Tweaks* and can be linear and rotational and are set to run over a timed period (duration).

How To: Add a Tweak

1. Drag the playhead (⬇) for the timeline to the required location.

2. In the *Presentation* tab>Component panel, click ⊞ (Tweak Components). Alternatively, right-click and select **Tweak Components**. The mini-toolbar opens.

3. In the Model Type drop-down list (shown in Figure 5–5), select whether a **Part** or **Component** will be tweaked. Use **Components** to select subassemblies.

Model Type ──────▶
drop-down list

Figure 5–5

4. Select a component or multiple components to be tweaked.
   • Press and hold <Ctrl> and select components in the graphics window or from the expanded model list in the **Scene** node of the Model Browser to select multiple components.
   • Press and hold the <Shift> to select a range of components in the Model Browser.
   • Select individual components or use a window selection technique to select components in the graphics window.
   • To clear a selected component, press and hold <Ctrl> and select it a second time.
   • All selected components are highlighted in blue.

5. Select the type of tweak. A triad will display on a face of the first selected component, similar to that shown in Figure 5–6 for a Move Tweak.
   • Click **Move** in the mini-toolbar to move the selected component linearly in the X, Y, or Z directions.
   • Click **Rotate** in the mini-toolbar to rotate the selected components about the X, Y, or Z axis.

Figure 5–6

If multiple components have been selected for a Tweak, the triad displays on the first object that was selected.

The default direction on the triad is gold.

6. (Optional) Reposition the triad if it doesn't meet the orientation requirements for the tweak.

   - Click **Locate** in the mini-toolbar. Hover the cursor over a new face reference and once the required control point on the face highlights, click to relocate the triad.
   - Use **Local** or **World** in the mini-toolbar to orient the triad relative to the component's coordinate system or the assembly coordinate system, respectively.

7. Select the control handle on a triad and drag it to define the tweak, as shown in Figure 5–7. Alternatively, enter a specific value tweak's entry field.

   - Select an X, Y, or Z arrowhead to move linearly.
   - Select a XY, YZ, or XZ plane to move in a plane.
   - Select a rotation handle to rotate about the X, Y, or Z axes.

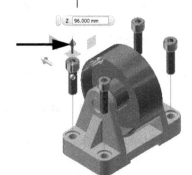

Arrowhead selected for linear tweak

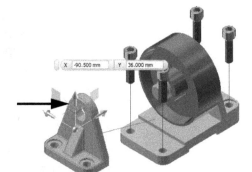

Plane selected for planar tweak

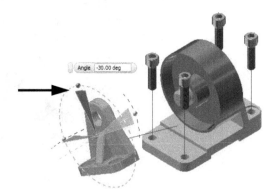

Rotation handle selected for rotational tweak

Figure 5–7

8. (Optional) Use the options in the *Trail* area of the mini-toolbar (shown in Figure 5–8) to control how the trail will be created.

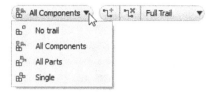

Figure 5–8

- In the drop-down list, select an option to add trails to all components in an assembly or subassembly (**All Components**) and all parts and a single trail for subassemblies (**All Parts**), a single trail for each group of selected components (**Single**), or no trail at all (**No Trails**).

- Select **Full Trail** to selectively remove or keep an entire trial or select **Trail Segment** to manipulate segments of the trail.

9. Continue to select additional triad handles to fully define the tweak or select additional components. Multiple combinations of handles and tweak types can be included.

10. Enter the **Duration** value for the tweak. The tweak will begin where the playhead was positioned and will run for the duration.

11. Complete the tweak operation:

- Click ✓ to complete the tweak.

- Click ✗ to cancel the operation.

Tweaks are listed in the Storyboard panel and Model Browser as shown in Figure 5–9. In this example, multiple tweaks with trails were created.

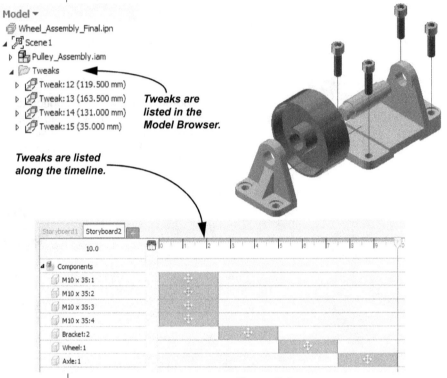

Figure 5–9

- In the Model Browser, the icons show whether the tweak is linear () or rotational ().

- In the Storyboard panel, the symbols used to identify the duration of the tweak indicates if it is linear or planar (), rotational (),or a combination of both ().

Repositioning/Moving Tweaks

A tweak's timeline entry can be dragged to reposition it on the timeline. To move multiple tweaks at once, press and hold <Ctrl> to select them prior to moving. The *Duration* of the tweaks can be changed by dragging its endline to the appropriate time.

Editing Tweaks

An existing tweak can be modified in any of the following ways:

- Change the translational or rotational values initially assigned to the tweak.

- Change the duration of the tweak.

- Control the visibility of the trail lines for a tweak.

New translational or rotational movements cannot be added to an existing tweak. A new tweak must be added.

How To: Edit a Tweak's values

1. Activate the **Edit Tweak** command.
   - In the timeline, right-click a tweak's symbol and select **Edit Tweak**.
   - In the graphic window, right-click a trail line that belongs to the tweak and select **Edit Tweak**.
   - In the Model Browser, expand the *Tweaks* folder, right-click a tweak, and select **Edit Tweak**.
   - Alternatively, double-click on the Tweak name or trail line to edit it.
2. Use the Tweak mini-toolbar to change the properties of the tweak.
   - Enter new values for the defined movements.
   - Press and hold <Ctrl> to add or remove components participating in the tweak.
   - Use the **Trail Line** options on the mini-toolbar to edit them.
   - Note that the duration cannot be edited using **Edit Tweak**.
3. Complete the edit:

   - Click ✓ to complete the edit.

   - Click ✕ to cancel the operation.

The Tweaks listed in the Model Browser are context sensitive. When in an animation storyboard, the tweaks belonging to the storyboard display. When editing a Snapshot View, only its tweaks display.

How To: Edit the Duration of a Tweak

1. In the timeline, right-click a tweak's symbol and select **Edit Time**. Alternatively, double-click on the Tweak symbol in the timeline.
2. Enter a new *Start*, *End* time, or *Duration* for the tweak in the mini-toolbar, as shown in Figure 5–10.

Figure 5–10

You can select multiple tweaks and edit their duration at the same time.

3. Complete the edit:

   • Click ✓ to complete the edit.

   • Click ✕ to cancel the operation.

Trail Visibility

Tweaks that contain trail lines can be manipulated once they are created to clear their visibility.

It is a recommended best practice to add trail lines during tweak creation and hide them, as required, after the fact.

• In the graphic window, right-click a trail line and select **Hide Trail Segment**, as shown in Figure 5–11. Using this method you can clear the trail segment for the individually selected trail line using the **Current** option or clear all trail lines in the group using the **Group** option.

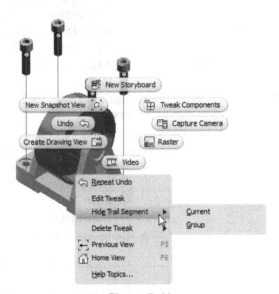

Figure 5–11

• In the Model Browser, expand the *Tweaks* folder, right-click a tweak or its component and select **Hide Trails** or **Hide Trail Segment**, as shown in Figure 5–12. By accessing the command at the Tweak level, you control all trails in the group. By accessing it at the component level you can specify it the trail for the current component (**Current**) or all components in the group are to be cleared (**Group**).

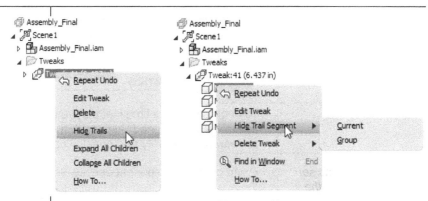

Figure 5–12

- Repeat the process using the Model Browser and use **Show Trail Segment** to return the display of trail lines to the model.

Deleting Tweaks

Similar to controlling the visibility of the trail lines in a tweak, you have multiple methods that can be used to delete individual and groups of tweaks from a presentation.

- In the graphic window, right-click a trail line and select **Delete Tweak**. Using this method, you can delete the tweak for the selected trail line using the **Current** option or delete all tweaks in the group using the **Group** option.

- In the Model Browser, expand the *Tweaks* folder, right-click a tweak and select **Delete**. All tweaks in the group are deleted.

- In the Model Browser, expand the *Tweaks* folder and **Tweak** node, right-click a component and select **Delete**.

- In the timeline, right-click on the tweak symbol and select **Delete**. You can specify it the Tweak for the current component (**Current**) or all components in the group are to be deleted (**Group**).

> **Hint: Aligning Start/End Time**
>
> To quickly align two Tweaks to either start or end at the same time, select them using <Ctrl>, right-click, and select **Align Start Time** or **Align End Time**.

Actions

Actions can be added to the timeline of a storyboard to control the appearance of components throughout an animation, or a camera position.

Model Appearance

To begin, place the timeliner playhead at the location that the action will be assigned. Actions that customize the model's appearance (visibility and opacity) can be added as follows:

*If a component was set as **Transparent** in the source assembly, that setting is visible if used in a presentation.*

- To change component opacity, select the component, and in the Component panel, click ⊞ (Opacity). Use the Opacity mini-toolbar (shown in Figure 5–13) to specify the opacity value. You can use the slider or enter a value in the entry field. Click ✓ to complete the modification. Opacity actions are identified with the ▢ symbol in the timeline and are initially set as instant actions.

Figure 5–13

- To clear the visibility of a component, select the component in the graphic window or Model Browser, right-click and select **Visibility**. This removes the component from display in the animation at the point where the playhead was located.

  Visibility actions are identified with the ▢ symbol in the timeline and can only be instantaneous.

*Multiple Opacity settings can be modified at the same time by preselecting them prior to selecting **Edit Opacity**.*

- To modify a Visibility or Opacity action, move the playhead to its location on the timeline, select the component, and use the **Opacity** and **Visibility** options a second time.

*The **Edit Time** option for a Visibility action only enables you to change the time to an exact value. You cannot set a Visibility action for a duration. If the visibility is to be returned, move the playhead to the time, and toggle on the component's visibility.*

- By default, an Opacity action is set to be instantaneous; however, it can be modified to run over a specified duration.

  To edit the action, right-click the ⬜ symbol in the timeline and select **Edit Time**. In the drop-down list, change the action type to **Duration**, as shown in Figure 5–14.

Figure 5–14

- Select and drag a Visibility or Opacity action along the timeline to relocate them.

- To delete a Visibility or Opacity action, select it in the timeline, right-click, and select **Delete**.

Camera Position

An action that changes the camera position can be set to run over a specified duration. To begin, place the timeliner playhead at the location that the action will be assigned.

How To: Customize the Model's Camera Position

1. To change position of the camera, use the ViewCube or other navigation tools to change the model orientation (camera).

2. In the Camera panel, click 🖥 (Capture Camera).

   - The action is added to the top of the timeline at the point where the playhead was positioned, as shown in Figure 5–15. It is created to run for 2.5secs.

The Camera Position action may look compressed at the top of the timeline if the timeline is not large enough and is showing the scroll bar.

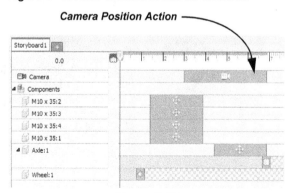

Figure 5–15

*Alternatively, you can right-click on a Camera Position action in the timeline and select **Edit Time** to open the mini-toolbar.*

- By default, the action is added as a Duration action. To make a change to the default duration (2.5 sec) or change it to an Instant action, double-click the camera action on the timeline. Using the mini-toolbar (shown in Figure 5–16), you can change the type of action and its *Start, End,* or *Duration* times.

Figure 5–16

- Select and drag a Camera Position action to move it along the timeline.

- To delete a Camera Position action, select it in the timeline, right-click, and select **Delete**.

Hint: Scratch Zone

The area on the timeline that displays prior to the start of the timeline is called the *Scratch Zone*. It is identified with the symbol, as shown in Figure 5–17. The *Scratch Zone* enables you to set the initial view settings, visibility, opacity, and camera position for the assembly. When the settings are made in the *Scratch Zone*, they are not included in the animation. It simply defines how the assembly displays at time 0 on the timeline.

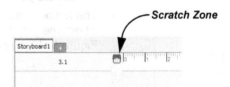

Figure 5–17

- To set the options, position the playhead of the timeliner in this area, and use the **Visibility**, **Opacity** and **Capture Camera** options, as required.

- Modifications cannot be made to the actions in the *Scratch Zone*. Use the **Visibility**, **Opacity** and **Capture Camera** options a second time to reset them.

Hint: Deleting all Actions for a Component

Individual Tweaks and Actions can be deleted directly on the timeline. To delete all actions associated with a component, right-click on the component name in the Storyboard panel and select **Delete Actions**.

- If the current storyboard was created using **Start from end of Previous**, the **Delete Actions** option will delete all current and inherited actions from the previous storyboard.

Playing a Storyboard

Once you have created an animation and have added actions, you can use the Timeline Controls to playback the entire storyboard. The Timeline Controls are located at the top of the Storyboard panel. The options in this panel are consistent with standard playback controls (rewind to beginning, play, pause, play in reverse, and fast forward to end).

Hint: Tweak and Action Selection

To quickly select all or multiple timeline entries for editing before or after a specific entry, right-click on the entry and select **Select>All Before** or **Select>All After**. When working with groups, right-click on one entry and select **Select>Group** to select all entries in the group.

5.3 Snapshot Views

Snapshot views store a combination of component display settings and positions in one view to communicate specific information in the model. The Snapshot view can be used to create image files for presentations or views in an Inventor drawing file. To create an exploded assembly view in a drawing you must create an exploded Snapshot view and reference it in a drawing.

The component display settings that can be assigned in a Snapshot view are similar to those used to create animations. They include:

- Component positions using tweaks
- Component visibility settings
- Component opacity settings
- Camera positions defined by the model's orientation
- View settings using the *View* tab.

A Snapshot view can be created using a previously created storyboard or they can be created independently.

Creating Snapshots from a Storyboard

How To: Create a Snapshot View from a Storyboard

1. Activate the scene to which the Snapshot view will be added.
   - To activate it, double click the scene name in the Model Browser.
2. In the Timeline, position the playhead at the point at which the Snapshot view is required.
3. In the Workshop panel, click ⬚ (New Snapshot View).

A new view is added in the Snapshot Views browser. The component display settings that exist in the storyboard at the location of the playhead are used in the Snapshot view.

- The ⬒ marker displays on the Snapshot view's thumbnail image, indicating that it is associated with the storyboard animation, as shown in Figure 5–18.

- The ⬒ marker also displays on the Timeline, indicating that a Snapshot view was created, as shown in Figure 5–18. The symbol can be dragged to change the snapshot location on the timeline, if required.

*To rename a Snapshot view, right-click on its thumbnail image and select **Rename**. Enter a new descriptive name for the image and press <Enter>.*

- If the Snapshot view marker is moved on the timeline or changes are made to any of the actions at that time, the ⊘ symbol displays on the view in the Snapshot Views browser, indicating that it is out of date. Select the symbol to update it.

Snapshot in the Snapshot Browser

Snapshot view

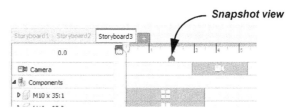

View 1

Figure 5–18

Hint: Snapshot Views at the Beginning of an Animation

Snapshot views that are created when the playhead is at the beginning of the animiation's timeline (0 seconds) will not create a dependent Snapshot view.

Creating Independent Snapshots

How To: Create an Independent Snapshot View

1. Activate the scene to which the Snapshot view will be added.
   - To activate it, double click the scene name in the Model Browser.
2. Position the Storyboard playhead in the *Scratch Zone*, as shown in Figure 5–19.
   - If an animation or actions exist in the Storyboard, position the playhead in the *Scratch Zone*.
   - If no animation or actions exist, independent Snapshot views will be created regardless of being in the *Scratch Zone*.

*To rename a Snapshot view, right-click on its thumbnail image and select **Rename**. Enter a new descriptive name for the image and press <Enter>.*

Scratch Zone

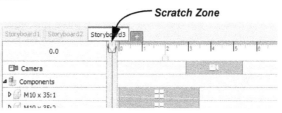

Figure 5–19

3. In the Workshop panel, click ⌐🔲¬ (New Snapshot View). The view is added to the Snapshot Views browser. The ⌂ marker does not display on the view's thumbnail image as it does for dependent views.

Editing a Snapshot View

Snapshot views that are dependent on the Storyboard show the assembly at a specific time on the timeline. In the case of independent views, they will likely need to be customized once the view is created.

How To: Edit an Independent Snapshot View

1. Activate the scene to which the Snapshot view exists.
2. In the Snapshot Views browser, right-click the view that is to be edited and select **Edit**. Alternatively, double-click the view to edit it. The *Edit View* tab becomes the active tab (shown in Figure 5–20) and the Storyboard panel is removed from the display.

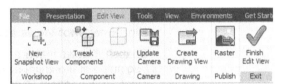

Figure 5–20

As you edit an existing view, you can click

(New Snapshot View) in the Workshop to create an additional view.

3. Set the component's view display using any of the following tools:

   - Use the ViewCube and Navigation bar to set the model orientation. Click (Update Camera) to update the view.
   - Select components, right-click, and clear the **Visibility** option for components that are not required in the view.
   - Select component(s) and on the Component panel, click (Opacity) to assign an Opacity value to component(s) in the view.
   - In the *View* tab, assign view settings from the *View* tab to customize the view.
   - Use the (Tweak Components) command to move or rotate components in the Snapshot view. Use the mini-toolbar in the same way as is done for an animation to move and rotate components in the view.

4. Click (Finish Edit View) to complete the edit.

Hint: Making a Dependent Snapshot View Independent

The ⬟ marker on a Snapshot view's thumbnail image indicates that it is associated (linked) with the storyboard animation. If you edit this type of view, you will be prompted that you can't make changes to a view that is linked to the timeline (as shown in Figure 5–21). To permanently break the link, click **Break Link**.

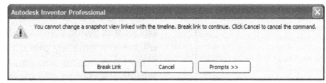

Figure 5–21

The ⬟ marker is removed from the Snapshot view's thumbnail image. Only the addition of a tweak or the change of Opacity and Visibility for a component require you to break the link. Changes to the camera position/orientation are permitted without breaking the link.

Creating a Drawing View from a Snapshot View

Creating drawings will be discussed in more detail later in the student guide.

Any of the Snapshot views listed in the Snapshot Views browser can be used to create a drawing view.

- The Snapshot view's name can be selected in the *Presentation* area of the Drawing View dialog box when an .IPN file is selected as the drawing model, as shown in Figure 5–22.

Figure 5–22

- A drawing view can also be created directly from the Presentation file using the following:

  - In the Snapshot Views browser, right-click on the thumbnail image and select **Create Drawing View**. The drawing view will be created using this Snapshot view.

- While editing a Snapshot view, in the *Edit View* tab> Drawing panel, click ⬛ (Create Drawing View). The drawing view will be created using this Snapshot view.

- In the *Presentation* tab>Drawing panel, click ⬛ (Create Drawing View). The drawing view will be created and defaults to using the first Snapshot view. You can select an alternate, if required.

Once the command is selected, you will be prompted to select a drawing template for the new drawing and then you will be immediately placed in the drawing. The Drawing View dialog box opens and you can begin to place the Base view and any additional Projected views, as shown in Figure 5–23.

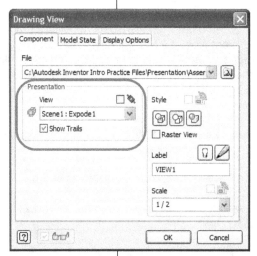 

Figure 5–23

The *Presentation* area of the dialog box displays the name of the Snapshot view being used. Consider the following:

- Select an alternate Snapshot view in the drop-down list.

- Show or clear the trails in the view using **Show Trails**. Trails can only be controlled if they exist in the Snapshot view.

- Select ⬛ to set the new view as associative. This ensures that if a change is made to the Snapshot view in the Presentation file, it will update the drawing view.

5.4 Publishing a Presentation File

Both Snapshot views and Storyboards can be published to various formats. Snapshot views can be published as raster images and Storyboards can be published as animations.

How To: Publish Snapshot Views

1. Activate the scene in which the Snapshot will be published.
2. Select the view(s) to publish in the Snapshot Views browser.
   - To publish multiple Snapshot views, press and hold <Ctrl> during selection.

A Snapshot view can be published while it is being edited by selecting  *(Raster) in the Edit View tab.*

3. Open the Publish to Raster Images dialog box, as shown in Figure 5–24 to publish the snapshots.
   - In the *Presentation* tab>Publish panel, click ▦ (Raster).
   - Right-click a view in the Snapshot Views browser and select **Publish to Raster**.

Figure 5–24

4. In the Publish to Raster Images dialog box. define the scope of publishing using the *Publish Scope* area.
   - Click **All Views** to publish all Snapshot views available in active scene.
   - Use **Selected Views** to publish the views that were previously selected.

5. In the *Image Resolution* area define the image size.
   - Use **Current Document Window Size** in the drop-down list to publish the view as it is currently displayed.
   - Select a predefined image size in the drop-down list.
   - Select **Custom** in the drop-down list and enter a custom *Width*, *Height*, and *Resolution* value by pixel or unit size.
   - Enter a *Resolution* value.
6. In the *Output* area, specify a folder to save the file. The Snapshot view name will be used as the published filename.
7. In the File Format drop-down list, select a publishing format.
8. Enable **Transparent Background**, if required.
9. Click **OK** to publish the image.

The supported image file formats include BMP, GIF, JPEG, PNG, or TIFF.

How To: Publish a Storyboard

1. Activate the scene in which the Storyboard will be published.
2. In the Storyboard panel, select the *Storyboard* tab that is to be published.
3. Open the Publish to Video dialog box, as shown in Figure 5–25 to publish the snapshots.

   - In the *Presentation* tab>Publish panel, click (Video).
   - Right-click a *Storyboard* tab and select **Publish**.

*The **Video** option is only available if an animation exists in the Storyboard panel.*

Figure 5–25

4. In the Publish to Video dialog box, define the scope of publishing using the *Publish Scope* area.

   • Use **All Storyboard** to publish all storyboards available in active scene.

   • Use **Current Storyboard** to publish the active storyboard.

   • Use **Current Storyboard Range** to publish a time range in the active storyboard. Enter values in the *From* and *To* fields.

   • Click **Reverse** to publish the video in a reverse order (end to start).

5. In the *Video Resolution* area, define the video size.

   • Use **Current Document Window Size** in the drop-down list to publish the video as it is currently displayed.

   • Select a predefined video size in the drop-down list.

   • Select **Custom** in the drop-down list and enter a custom *Width*, *Height*, and *Resolution* value by pixel or unit size.

6. In *Output* area, specify a name for the video and a folder to save the file.

The supported video file formats include WMV and AVI. A WMV video player must be installed on your computer to publish to WMV format.

7. In the File Format drop-down list, select a publishing format.

8. Click **OK** to publish the video.

9. For AVI formatted videos, select a video compressor and set compression quality, if available. Click **OK**.

Practice 5a

Create an Animation

Practice Objectives

- Create a new presentation file using a standard template.
- Create an animation that explodes the components of an assembly using translational and rotational movements.
- Control the visual display and orientation of components in an animation.
- Play an animation and then publish it.

In this practice, you will create a presentation file using a wheel assembly. The assembly file that will be used is shown in Figure 5–26. Using the tools in the Presentation file, you will create an animation that explodes the components of the assembly to show how it is assembled.

*A video called **video2.avi** has been provided in the Presentation folder of the practice files folder for you to review what will be done in this practice. This video used compression to reduce the file size, so the quality of the video is impacted.*

Figure 5–26

Task 1 - Create a presentation file.

*Alternatively, use the Quick Access toolbar, **File** menu, or the My Home tab to create a new file.*

1. In the *Get Started* tab>Launch panel, click ☐ (New).

2. Select the *Metric* folder, select **Standard(mm).ipn** in the Create New File dialog box to create a new presentation file, and click **Create**.

   - You might need to scroll down in the list to locate this template.

*If a specific representation of the file is to be used, click **Options** and select the required Design View, Level of Detail, or Positional Representation to use.*

3. In the Insert dialog box, navigate to the *Presentation* folder and select **Wheel_Assembly.iam**. Click **Open**.

   - The presentation environment displays and the *Presentation* tab is the active tab.
   - By default, there is a single scene created using the wheel assembly and **Storyboard1** is active. No snapshots are initially created.

Task 2 - Define the initial model display for the animation.

The Scratch Zone is where you can set the initial visibility, opacity, and camera position for the model.

1. The playhead ( ) starts at time 0secs. Drag the playhead to the left into the (Scratch Zone) area of the panel, as shown in Figure 5–27.

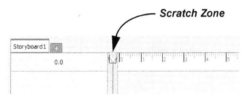

Figure 5–27

Component visibility and opacity can also be set in the Scratch Zone to define the model's initial display.

2. Rotate the model into a custom orientation using the ViewCube. Select the corner shown in Figure 5–28. This positions the model for the start of the animation.

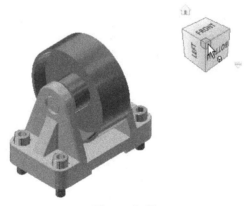

Figure 5–28

3. In the Camera panel, click (Capture Camera). This stores the orientation for the start position of the animation.

Task 3 - Create an exploded animation of the assembly.

1. Expand the **Scene1** node in the Model Browser and the **Wheel_Assembly.iam** node. All of the assembly component's names display. This provides a convenient way to select components.

2. To move components, in the *Presentation* tab>Component panel, click (Tweak Components). The Tweak Component mini-toolbar opens as shown in Figure 5–29.

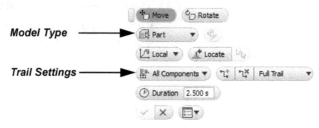

Model Type

Trail Settings

Figure 5–29

3. Ensure that **Part** is selected in the Model Type drop-down list.

4. Press and hold <Ctrl> and select the four **M10 x 35** components in the Model Browser. All the components should be highlighted in the model and the tweak triad should be displayed.

5. Ensure that **Move** is selected in the top row of the mini-toolbar to move components in either the X, Y, or Z directions.

6. Expand the Trail Settings drop-down list in the mini-toolbar. The options in this field enables you to customize if trails are created. In this practice, they will be created and you will later learn how to quickly toggle them on and off. Ensure that **All Components** is selected.

7. The triad orientation displays the local coordinate system for the part. Expand the **Local** option and select **World** to change the orientation of the triad to be consistent with the assembly coordinate system.

*Alternatively, you can use the **Select Other** tool in the graphics window to select any hidden components to avoid rotating the model and changing its orientation in the animation.*

8. Select the arrow that points in the Z direction relative to the assembly's origin, as shown in Figure 5–30.

   - If the model origin is not displayed, consider toggling it on in the Application Options>*Display* tab>**Show Origin 3D indicator**.

Depending on the order in which the components are selected, the triad may display in a different location.

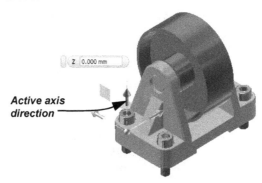

Figure 5–30

9. The active Z axis direction displays in gold. Drag the arrowhead upwards to move the four components. Enter **75** in the Z entry field to move the components a specific distance.

10. Click [✓] to complete the Tweak and close the mini-toolbar.

Tweak actions are set at 2.5 seconds by default. This can be modified in the Tweak mini-toolbar prior to closing it or it can be modified after it is created.

11. Note that the four components are listed in the Storyboard panel and the tweak actions are scheduled to last 2.5 secs, as shown in Figure 5–31.

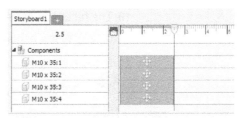

Figure 5–31

12. Hover the cursor over the Tweak action ([⊞]) for the first component in the list, right-click, and select **Edit Time**.

13. In the mini-toolbar, set the *Duration* value to **3.00**. Click .

14. The first component is now set to get into its exploded position slower than the others. Click ◄ in the playback controls to rewind the timeline to the beginning and click ▷. Note the differences in the timing.

15. Hover the cursor over the Tweak action ( ) for the second component in the list and double-click to edit it. This is an alternative method to edit the timing.

16. Set the *Duration* value to **3.00**. Click ✓.

17. For the third component, hover the cursor over the right-hand edge of the action bar. Drag to the right to manually extend its duration. Ensure that it snaps to 3secs.

18. Extend the duration of the fourth component using any of the methods described. The Storyboard panel should display as shown in Figure 5–32.

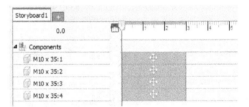

Figure 5–32

19. The fasteners have not been moved high enough. Right-click on any of the actions ( ) and select **Edit Tweak**.

20. In the *Distance* field, enter **140mm** as the new value. Click ✓. Because they are a group, they all are edited together.

Task 4 - Add additional tweaks to components.

---

1. Click ◄ to move the playhead to the end of the current actions. This ensures that the next tweak is added immediately at the end of the last tweak.

2. In the Component panel, click 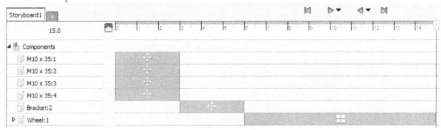 (Tweak Components). Using the following table move and rotate the Bracket and Wheel components. The Storyboard timeline and component display should display as shown in Figure 5–33 after the two components are tweaked. Use the Global coordinate system when tweaking the components.

Ensure that the playhead is at the correct position on the timeline when defining each tweak.

Component	Tweaks
Bracket:2	• Translate -175mm along the X-axis. • Define the tweak as 3.00 secs.
Wheel	• Translate -110 mm along the X-axis. • Translate 120 mm along the Z axis. • Rotate 90 degrees in the XZ plane. • Modify each tweak to 3.00 secs, if not already set.

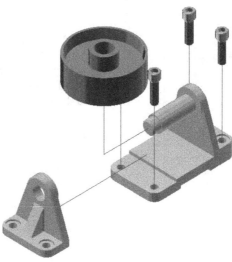

Figure 5–33

3. Play the animation from the beginning and note how the wheel is unassembled with three actions that occur consecutively. After playing, note that the model displays reassembled. This is only because the playhead returns to where it starts on the timeline. The animation will end fully disassembled at 15 seconds once published.

4. The three actions for the Wheel are grouped. In the Storyboard, expand the **Wheel** component in the component list to show the individual actions. To manipulate them, it must be expanded.

5. Manipulate the duration of the rotation action ( ) and relocate it on the timeline such that it occurs while the component is moving in the Z direction, similar to that shown in Figure 5–34.

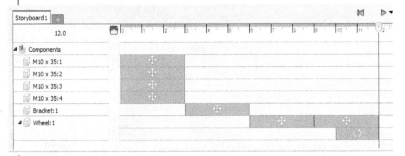

Figure 5–34

6. Use the following table to apply tweaks to the remaining components. The component display should display as shown in Figure 5–35 after the remaining three components are tweaked. Use the Global coordinate system when tweaking the components.

Ensure that the playhead is at the correct position on the timeline when defining each tweak.

Component	Tweaks
Axle	• Translate -110mm along the X-axis. • Define the tweak as 3.00 secs.
Bracket:1	• Translate 110mm along the X-axis. • Define the tweak as 2.50 secs.
Plate	• Translate -80 mm along the Z axis. • Define the tweak as 2.50 secs.

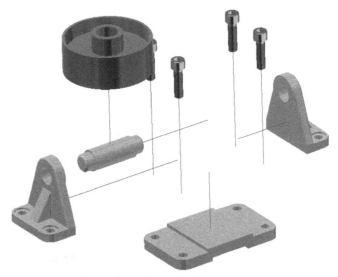

Figure 5–35

7. Manipulate the timeline such that the last two components assemble at the same time and run for 2.00 seconds.

8. Play the animation and verify that it functions as expected.

   • A video called **video1.avi** has been provided in the practice files folder for you to compare with. This video used compression to reduce file size, so the quality of the video is impacted.

9. Save the presentation file using its default name into the *Presentation* folder.

Task 5 - Incorporate visual changes in the animation.

1. In the Model Browser, right-click on the *Tweaks* folder and select **Hide All Trails**, as shown in Figure 5–36.

If you were to expand the Tweaks folder, it lists all tweaks that were created and you can individually edit them or hide their trail lines.

Figure 5–36

2. Return the playhead to the beginning of the timeline and play the animation. Note that the trail lines are all removed from the display.

3. Once the fasteners are exploded, they can fade from the display. Place the playhead at **3s** and select all four fasteners.

4. In the Component panel, click (Opacity). When prompted that the scene is associated with a design view and that you must break or override the associativity, click **Break**. This makes the scene independent of the Master Design View that was imported into the scene.

5. On the mini-toolbar, drag the *Opacity* slider to **0**. Click ☑.

6. Note how the new component opacity action is grouped with the other actions for these components. Expand the first component, as shown in Figure 5–37.

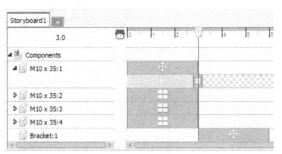

Figure 5–37

7. Right-click on the ☐ action for the first fastener and select **Edit Time**. By default, the action is created as an Instant action.

8. Select **Duration** in the drop-down list in the mini-toolbar.

9. Set the *Start* value to **2.50** and the *End* value to **3.5**. Click ☑.

10. Play the animation and note the difference between the first fastener's visibility changes and the other fasteners.

As an alternative to using opacity, you could have also cleared the visibility of the components at a specific time. The Visibility action is only instantaneous.

11. Modify the other three fasteners such that they also fade out over a duration of 2.50 to 3.50secs.

12. Compress the **M10 x 35** component nodes in the Storyboard panel once your edits are complete.

Task 6 - Spin the model at the end of the animation.

1. Click ▷◁ to move the playhead to the end of the animation.

2. Return the model to its default Home view using the ViewCube and zoom in on the model.

3. In the Camera panel, click 💾 (Capture Camera). A camera action is added to the top of the timeline.

4. Modify the length of the camera action by right-clicking on the 🎥 symbol and selecting **Edit Time**.

5. Modify the duration to start at 16 seconds and last until 19 seconds. Alternatively, you can drag the action and extend its action on the timeline.

6. Move the playhead to the beginning of the animation. The entire timeline should display similar to that shown in Figure 5–38.

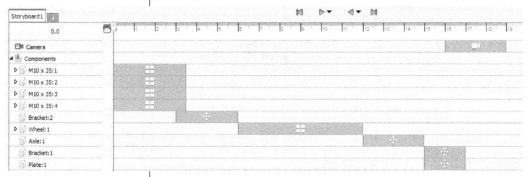

Figure 5–38

7. Play the animation to see how this new Camera action affects the animation.

Task 7 - Modify the View settings in the model.

The settings that are set in the View tab are temporary and are not saved with the Presentation file.

1. Return the playhead into the *Scratch Zone* once again.

2. On the ribbon, select the *View* tab. Use the tools in the Appearance panel to set the following:

   - In the Shadows drop-down list, enable **Ambient Shadows**.
   - In the Visual Style drop-down list, select **Technical Illustration** or an alternate style. Note that threads do not display in a technical illustration.

3. Play the animation.

Task 8 - Publish the Storyboard.

1. In the *Presentation* tab>Publish panel, click (Video). Alternatively, right-click on the *Storyboard1* tab and select **Publish**.

2. In the Publish to Video dialog box, ensure that **Current Storyboard** is selected in the *Publish Scope* area.

3. In the *Video Resolution* area, maintain the **Current Document Window Size** option to publish the video as it is currently displayed.

4. In the *Output* area, set the video name to **my_wheel_assembly** and save it to the *Presentation* folder in the practice files folder.

5. In the File Format drop-down list, select **AVI File (*.avi)**.

6. Click **OK** to publish the video.

7. If time permits, publish the video as uncompressed, otherwise, select a video compressor type and assign a compression quality. Click **OK**.

8. Navigate to the *Presentation* folder in the practice files and play the video once it has published.

   - A video called **video2.avi** has been provided in the practice files folder for you to compare with. This video used compression to reduce file size so the quality of the video is impacted.

9. Save the presentation file and close the window.

Practice 5b | Create Snapshots

Practice Objectives

- Create snapshots that are dependent on a storyboard animation.
- Create snapshots that are independent from a storyboard animation.
- Edit snapshots to manipulate component position and component display.
- Update snapshots that are dependent on a storyboard animation.

In this practice, you will create Snapshot views that are both dependent on an animation as well as independent of it. You will also learn how to edit both types of Snapshot views using the tools available in the Presentation environment. The independent exploded Snapshot view is shown in Figure 5–39.

Figure 5–39

Task 1 - Create Snapshot Views that are dependent on a Storyboard animation.

In this task you will create multiple Snapshot views all based on the storyboard animation that already exists in the presentation file.

1. Continue working with the Presentation file from the previous practice or open **Wheel_Assembly_Final.ipn** from the *Presentation* folder.

2. Note that there is currently one scene in the file (**Scene1**) and that this scene does not currently have any Snapshot views in the Snapshot Views browser.

3. In the timeline, move the playhead to the beginning of the animation (0secs). You can select ◀ or simply drag the playhead to the beginning of the animation.

4. In the Workshop panel, click ⌐🔲¬ (New Snapshot View).

5. **View1** is added to the Snapshot Views browser. Right-click on the **View1** thumbnail image and select **Rename**. Set the new name to **Fully Assembled**.

6. Move the playhead to approximately 2.5secs. This should show the fasteners exploded, but not yet set to an Opacity value of 0.

7. In the Workshop panel, click ⌐🔲¬ (New Snapshot View).

8. **View2** is added to the Snapshot Views browser. The ⬒ marker displays on the Snapshot view's thumbnail image, indicating that it is associated with the storyboard animation. Snapshot views created at 0secs are not associative to the storyboard.

9. Select the view label for the **View2** thumbnail image. Set the new name to **Step1**. This is an alternative to using the **Rename** command.

Snapshot views can also be created by right-clicking on the playhead in the timeline.

10. Using the steps previously described, create the following snapshots. The Snapshots Views browser should display similar to that shown Figure 5–40.

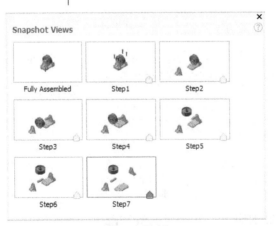

Time (seconds)	Snapshot View Name
6	Step2
9	Step3
10	Step4
12	Step5
15	Step6
17	Step7

Figure 5–40

11. Refer to the Snapshot Views browser and the Storyboard timeline and note the following:

- The ⬢ marker that displays on the last view (**Step7**) is blue and the outline of the view is also blue, indicating that the view is active.

- The ⬡ markers displays along the timeline, showing the locations where the snapshots were taken.

Task 2 - Modify a dependent snapshot view.

Between 15s and 17s both the second **Bracket** and the **Plate** are moved apart. For static images, only the **Bracket** needs to be moved. The animation is to stay as it is; however, you will edit the Step 7 view to make the change.

1. Right-click on the **Step7** thumbnail image and select **Edit**. The *Edit View* tab is activated, as shown in Figure 5–41

Figure 5–41

2. Select the **Plate** component in the graphics window. Right-click and select **Delete Tweak>Last**.

3. When prompted that you can't make changes to a view that is linked to the timeline, click **Break Link** to permanently break the link. The **Plate** component returns to its original position. No other changes are required in this view.

4. In the Exit panel, click ✔ (Finish Edit View).

5. Note that the **Step7** view no longer has the ⬢ marker. This indicates that it is now an independent view.

Task 3 - Modify actions on the timeline.

1. In the timeline, expand the four **M10 x 35** components.

2. Right-click on the ⊠ symbol for the first component, right-click and select **Delete**, as shown in Figure 5–42. The first fastener is returned to the model display.

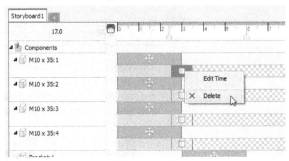

Figure 5–42

3. Delete the three other Opacity actions for the other fasteners. To delete the three fasteners at once, press and hold <Ctrl> to select them prior to selecting **Delete**. Five of the Snapshot views that are dependent on the timeline now show the

   ⊘ symbol on their thumbnail image, as shown in Figure 5–43.

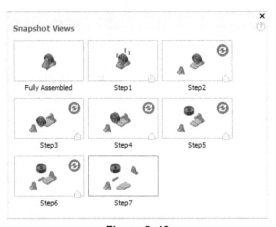

Figure 5–43

4. Select the ⊘ symbol on each thumbnail image to update them to reflect the change in the animation.

Task 4 - Modify the orientation of a model in a Snapshot view.

1. Double-click on the **Step6** thumbnail image in the Snapshot Views browser to edit it.

2. Using the ViewCube, rotate the model into an alternate position so that you can see all of the fasteners. In the Camera panel, click ⬚ (Update Camera). Note that the view changes in the thumbnail image and you were not prompted that the change would require you to break the link to the animation. Camera position changes do not affect the associativity with the animation.

3. In the Exit panel, click ✔ (Finish Edit View).

Task 5 - Create an independent view.

In this task, you will create a new Snapshot view that is independent of the timeline. You will then explode the assembly to create an alternate explode view that can be used in a drawing.

1. In the timeline, move the playhead to the beginning of the animation (0secs).

2. Create a new Snapshot view and rename it to **Exploded View**.

3. Edit the new Exploded View.

For more detail on tweaking components, refer to Practice 20a.

4. Rotate the model and use the 🔳 (Tweak Components) command to explode the components similar to that shown in Figure 5–44.

   • When creating the exploded view, create it with visible trail lines.

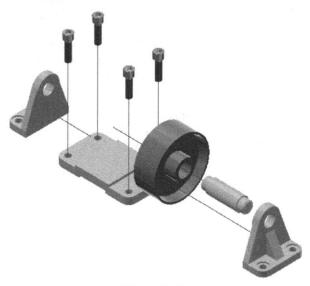

Figure 5–44

5. In the Camera panel, click 🖫 (Update Camera).

6. Finish the edit to return to the *Presentation* tab.

7. Save the presentation file and close the window.

> **Hint: Creating a drawing view from a Snapshot view.**
>
> A Snapshot view can be created directly from a presentation file using the **Create Drawing View** option. Drawing views are discussed further in a later chapter.

Chapter Review Questions

1. Which of the following file formats is used to create an exploded assembly model in a Drawing view?

    a. .IAM

    b. .IPT

    c. .IPN

    d. .DWG

2. What is the purpose of a Presentation file? (Select all that apply.)

    a. To simplify the display of an assembly.

    b. To create an Exploded View of an assembly.

    c. To update an assembly more quickly.

    d. To create an animation of an assembly.

    e. To help document and visualize the assembly.

3. Which of the following statements are true regarding a Presentation file? (Select all that apply.)

    a. Once the Presentation template is selected for use, you are immediately prompted to open the model that will be used in **Scene1** of the presentation.

    b. A Snapshot view that is oriented in the model's Home view is automatically added to a new Presentation file.

    c. Multiple storyboards can be created in a presentation file to document an assembly.

    d. Storyboard animations can be used in a drawing view.

4. It is not possible to edit a Snapshot view that was created dependent on a specific time in an animation.

    a. True

    b. False

5. Which command enables you to save a specific view orientation at a set time in an animation?

    a. **New Storyboard**

    b. **New Snapshot View**

    c. **Tweak Components**

    d. **Capture Camera**

6. What is the purpose of adding a trail?

   a. To define a path for an animation.

   b. To move the position of a component.

   c. To change the color of a component.

   d. To help define the relationships between the components in terms of how they are assembled.

7. To create an animated assembly of a model's assembly process, you must create an animation that uses the _____ command.

   a. **New Storyboard**

   b. **Tweak Components**

   c. **Opacity**

   d. **Capture Camera**

8. Which of the following are valid methods to change the duration of an action in a storyboard animation? (Select all that apply.)

   a. Enter a *Duration* value in the mini-toolbar during Tweak creation.

   b. Use the **Edit Tweak** command and enter a new *Duration* value.

   c. Use the **Edit Time** command and enter a new *Duration* value.

   d. Drag the action's duration directly in the timeline.

9. **Move** and **Rotate** tweaks can be assigned to the same component at one time.

   a. True

   b. False

10. Which type of view setting is only be instantaneous when assigned to an animation?

   a. Opacity

   b. Visibility

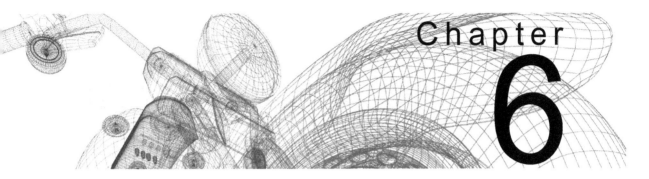

Chapter 6

Drawing Enhancements

In this chapter, you learn about the enhancements that have been introduced in the Autodesk® Inventor® software in both the 2016 and 2017 releases with respect to the Drawing environment. The enhancements that are discussed cover the changes to view creation and the changes made to the Annotation tools.

Learning Objectives in this Chapter

- Describe the enhancements that affect how drawings and their views are created.
- Describe the enhancements that have been incorporated into the drawing annotation tools and how they are used in a drawing.

6.1 View Enhancements

Creating a New Drawing

With the release of the Autodesk Inventor 2016 software, it is now possible to create a new drawing directly from a part or assembly file. It enables you to right-click on the model name node in the Model Browser and select **Create Drawing View**, as shown in Figure 6–1.

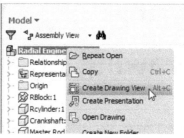

Figure 6–1

- Once the option is selected, you are prompted to select a drawing template and the temporary Base view is automatically placed in the drawing.

- The orientation of the model at the time of the drawing's creation is used as the default orientation for the new Base view.

Base & Projected Views

As of 2016, the process of creating a Base view in a drawing has been enhanced. To support this, the Drawing View dialog box has been changed, as shown in Figure 6–2.

Figure 6–2

Component Tab

- The visual display style icons have been updated. To set the view display, click:

  -  for hidden line

  - for no hidden line

  - for shaded

- The orientation controls for setting the Base view's orientation are no longer in the Drawing View dialog box. The preview that displays on the drawing sheet now contains green manipulators on the view border and a ViewCube (shown in Figure 6–3) to fully define the orientation, scale, and placement of the drawing view.

Figure 6–3

- Use the ViewCube to reorient the base view, as required. You can select alternate faces, edges, or corners on the ViewCube to reorient the model.

- Select on the ViewCube to reorient the model to its default isometric view.

- Select inside the view's frame and drag the view to reposition it on the sheet.

- Select the corner manipulator of the temporary view to scale the view.

- Select any of the eight small arrows that display around the view to place a projected view at a set distance from the Base view. Alternatively, you can drag off the Base view to place a Projected view at a specific location.

- Select ✕ on a placed projected view to delete it from the drawing before the views have been finalized.

- The expanded ViewCube options (▽) provide access to setting either Orthographic or Perspective views.

- To create a user-defined orientation, click 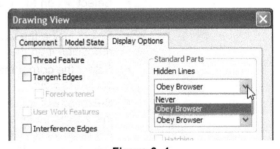 on the ViewCube and select **Custom View Orientation**. The controls are the same as those in previous versions of the Autodesk Inventor software.

Model State & Display Options tabs

The options on the *Model State* and *Display Options* tabs are similar to older versions; however, some of the commands have been reordered, regrouped, or removed, as follows: include:

- Drop-down lists have been incorporated on all tabs to help reduce the size of the Drawing View dialog box.

- The welding commands on the *Display Options* tab have been regrouped with the other weld options on the *Model State* tab.

- The **All Model Dimensions** option is now only visible for views that reference Part models.

- The **Show Trails** option is now included on the *Component* tab when a presentation is being added as a drawing view.

- Controls have been added to the *Display Options* tab to control the display of hidden lines in standard fasteners when views are set as hidden line. This affects any Content Center fasteners from the *Fasteners* and *Sheet Metal* folders. This has been done to help simplify the hidden line display in a view. To control this, set *Hidden Lines* in the *Standard Parts* area to **Never**. To include them, set the option to **Obey Browser**, as shown in Figure 6–4.

Figure 6–4

The creation of Projected views is now automatic after Base view creation and cannot be controlled with an option. To finalize the view after Base view placement, right-click and select **OK** or you can continue placing projected views.

Opening an Existing Drawing

The **Defer Updates** option in *Document Settings* enables you to suppresses automatic updates for the active drawing. To update the drawing, you must clear the option. As of Inventor 2017 (R2), when opening a drawing that has had the **Defer Updates** option (Document Settings) enabled, in addition to a warning message, you are now provided with options on how to handle the prompt, as shown in Figure 6–5.

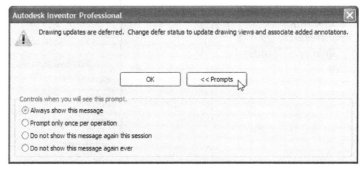

Figure 6–5

Section Views

With the release of the Autodesk Inventor 2017 software, it is now possible to define how the break lines for partially sectioned components will display. This is done using the options in the *Cut Edges* area. The options enable you to select a smooth () or jagged () break, as shown in Figure 6–6. The default option is **Smooth**.

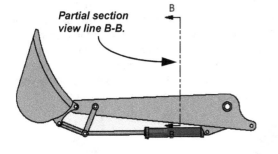

Partial section view line B-B.

SECTION B-B
SCALE 0.02

B-B was created using the Jagged cut edge option.

SECTION B-B
SCALE 0.02

B-B was created using the Smooth cut edge option.

Figure 6–6

• With the release of 2017 (R2), hatch patterns can now be set to display as solid. This is done by right-clicking on the hatch pattern and selecting **Edit**. In the Edit Hatch Pattern dialog box, select **SOLID** in the Pattern drop-down list, as shown in Figure 6–7.

*By default, the color of a solid hatch is black. To change it, you can edit its appearance in **Layers>Hatch** style in the Style and Standard Editor.*

Figure 6–7

Transparent Components

As of 2016, when working in an assembly model drawing view, you can set individual components to be transparent in a precise view (not raster). Setting it as transparent ensures that the component displays in a view, but prevents it from hiding the geometry of other components in the same view, as shown in Figure 6–8. To set a component as transparent in a drawing view, expand the Model Browser so that the assembly model for the drawing view displays and right-click on the component name and select **Transparent**. This is the same as how visibility of a component can be toggled on and off in a view.

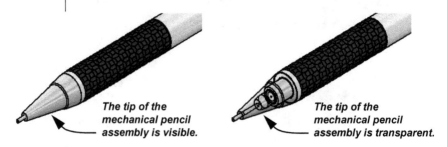

The tip of the mechanical pencil assembly is visible.

The tip of the mechanical pencil assembly is transparent.

Figure 6–8

Drawing Sketches

The following enhancements have been added to the 2016 software, which affect how you create and reference geometry in a sketch.

- In previous versions, to associate a sketch with a view you had to preselect the view prior to initiating the **Start Sketch** option. The workflow for starting a sketch has now been modified so that once the command has been activated, you can do any of the following:

  - Select an existing view to associate the sketch with the view.
  - Select on the sheet to add the sketch to the sheet.
  - Select an existing sketched entity to open the existing sketch and add to it.

- When creating a view sketch, the **Project Geometry** option now enables you to project any included work features that have been set to display in the view.

If a drawing sheet does not have any views or sketches on it, a sheet sketch is automatically started.

Printing Drawings

When batch printing drawing files using the Task Scheduler, it is now possible to schedule drawings with varying sizes to be printed at the same time. When setting up the printer settings for the task, you can set the new **Auto Size to Drawing Sheet Size option** in the Size drop-down list, as shown in Figure 6–9. This option ensures that the paper size and orientation defined in the drawing is used.

If the printer does not support the sheet size, the log file reports the names of the drawings that could not be printed.

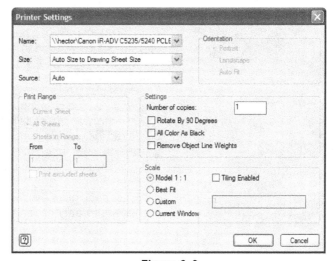

Figure 6–9

6.2 Annotation Enhancements

Sheet Properties

A new property called **Initial View Scale** was added to the *Sheet Property* category in 2016. Title blocks in all of the default drawing templates have been updated to include this new scale property. It automatically populates the **Scale** value that was assigned when creating the first drawing view. Additionally, you can use this property in any Text annotation by assigning the property, as shown in Figure 6–10.

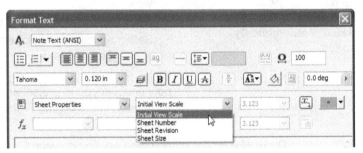

Figure 6–10

Tables

With the release of the Autodesk Inventor 2017 software, tables were enhanced to provide added flexibility when using them. The enhancements include the following:

- Headings will now automatically wrap when a column is resized. Additionally, columns can be resized to fit the largest word by double-clicking on its border in the table's editor. This adjustment is available in all tables (i.e, Parts Lists, Hole Tables, Rev Tables).

- For Parts List tables, you can now control how the parts list is filtered if you are creating a parts list for a design view. Prior to 2017 this was not possible and the full QTY values were displayed in the table regardless of the components shown in the design view. To enable Inventor to take into account the design view settings, you must edit the parts list table and in the Filter settings (🔳), enable the **Limit QTY to visible components only** option, as shown in Figure 6–11.

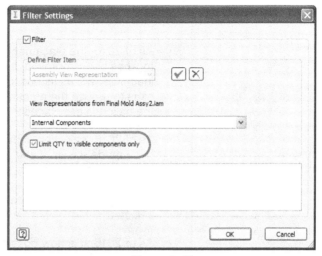

Figure 6–11

- A file can be opened directly from the Parts List dialog box or the table by right-clicking the model name and selecting **Open**. Files can also be opened directly from the Bill of Materials dialog box in a drawing. The **Open** options are shown in Figure 6–12.

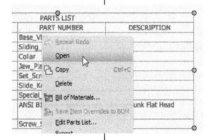 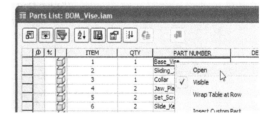

Figure 6–12

Revision Tables can also be exported to excel macro-enabled files.

- With the release of the Inventor 2017 (R2) software, Parts Lists can now be exported to an excel macro-enabled file (.XLSM), as shown in Figure 6–13.

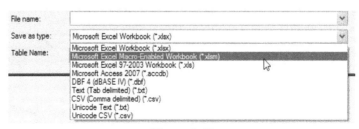

Figure 6–13

Balloons

The following enhancements have been made to the balloon functionality:

- As of 2016, the placement of balloons using the automatic tool has been improved. It defines the start point for a balloon leader as well as its position and length. This improvement aims to reduce the amount of repositioning necessary once the balloons are placed.

- As of 2016, selection of balloons for alignment purposes has been made easier. If you use a window selection box and linear entities from the view are selected, the **Align** options are still displayed when you right-click. Any linear entities are cleared from the selection box if an alignment option is selected.

- As of 2016, it is now possible to align balloons based on the selection of a reference edge that can define the direction. To do this, select the balloons to align, right-click, and select **Align>To Edge** in the context menu. Once the reference edge is selected, you can drag the balloons and place them as required while maintaining the edge alignment.

- As of 2016, the split balloon style has been corrected so that the split line extends fully to the circle, as shown in Figure 6–14. To update existing balloons, you must edit the style and reassign it, as they are not automatically updated when the drawing is migrated to 2016.

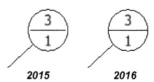

2015   2016

Figure 6–14

- As of 2017, a new rectangular balloon style has been added, as shown in Figure 6–15.

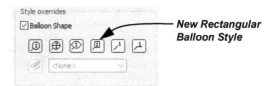

Figure 6–15

- As of 2016, custom balloon shapes are now included in the Balloon standard in the Style and Standard Editor, as shown in Figure 6–16. To assign this as the default balloon format for the drawing, select ✏ (User-defined Symbol) and then select the custom symbol. The symbol must exist in the *Sketch Symbols* category in the Drawing Resources to be available for selection. You must set this option in the drawing template files to ensure that all new drawings use a custom symbol as the default placement shape.

Figure 6–16

- As of 2017 (R2), stacked balloons can now be sorted, as shown in Figure 6–17. Previously, this option was not available. The sort options enable you to sort the balloons numerically from smallest (top) to largest (bottom) or to sort alphabetically from A (top) to Z (bottom).

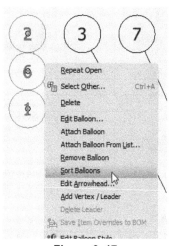

Figure 6–17

Text

The Text dialog box was enhanced with the 2016 release to add the use of additional text formatting tools. The updated dialog box is shown in Figure 6–18.

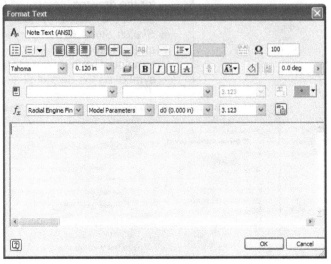

Figure 6–18

- Bullets, numbering, and strike-through formats can be used. When bullets or numbers are copied from Microsoft® Word, their formatting is recognized.

- Justification to the baseline of the text box when using the **Single Line Text** option.

- Text can be modified to be all caps, title case, or lower case once the text has been added.

- An enhanced symbol list has been added.

- A background fill color can be added to the text box. (This is new in 2017).

- The Zoom In and Zoom Out controls for enlarging the text in the text area have been removed. To change the display size of the text, place the cursor in the text area, hold <Ctrl>, and use the scroll wheel on the mouse to zoom in or out.

- Text is now immediately displayed on the drawing as a preview as you are typing in the text area. This enables you to make changes as you create the annotation.

- Leader and non-leader text can now be rotated, where previously only non-leader text could be rotated.

- You can now rotate non-leader text directly on the drawing sheet without using the Format Text dialog box. To do this, select the text and use the blue rotation grip to rotate the text as required, as shown in Figure 6–19.

Figure 6–19

Annotation Leaders

Enhancements in the 2016 version of the software have made working with leaders much easier to manipulate. These enhancements include leaders attached to dimensions, text, balloons, symbols, etc. and include the following:

- When placing an annotation feature that has a leader associated with it, you can now right-click once the command is active and select **Single-segment leader**, as shown in Figure 6–20 for Leader Text. Once set, you can begin creating the annotation and you are no longer required to right-click and select **Continue** if a single leader is required. This option is maintained until explicitly disabled and is independent for each annotation type.

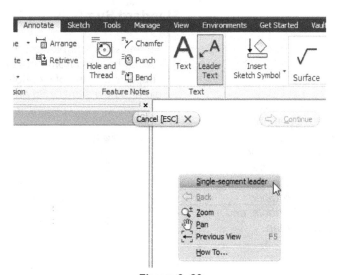

Figure 6–20

Similar to the new Balloon enhancement, when you use a window selection box, any items that are not leaders that can be aligned are automatically cleared from the selection box once an alignment option is selected.

- Leadered annotations can now be aligned horizontally, vertically, or based on a reference edge. To align, select the annotations, right-click and select **Align** to access the three alignment options shown in Figure 6–21.

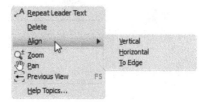

Figure 6–21

- The snapping behavior for leadered annotations has been reversed. When placing previously, annotations would snap automatically in 15 degree intervals, behavior which you could override by holding <Ctrl>. This has now been reversed. To enable snapping when placing an annotation, hold <Ctrl>.

Symbol Enhancements

With the released of the 2016 software, enhancements have been made to standard symbols and sketched symbols. These include:

Standard Symbols

- An enhanced graphical symbol list has been added. These can be inserted from any drawing annotation type that supports the use of symbols (e.g, text, dimensions, etc). The old and new symbol list are shown in Figure 6–22.

The 2016 symbols list is divided into five segments: Common Symbols, Geometric Characteristic, Material Removal Modifier, General Symbols, and Character Map.

2015

2016/2017

Figure 6–22

- Surface texture and feature control frame symbols have been updated to the latest standards. Additionally, the dialog boxes used to create these symbols have been enhanced to incorporate the standard changes and improve usability.

- A Pressed Joint weld symbol (工) is now available for use when adding a weld symbol annotation to a drawing. This option is only available once you enable it in the Style and Standard Editor's Welding Symbols filter list.

Sketched Symbols

The process of creating a sketched symbol in a drawing is the same as in previous versions of the software; however, some new enhancements were made in 2016 to make it easier to access the creation and insertion options. Additionally, changes were made to where symbols can be stored.

- The Symbols panel on the *Annotate* tab has been modified (as shown in Figure 6–23) so that you can now easily select the options for creating a new symbol or inserting an existing symbol.

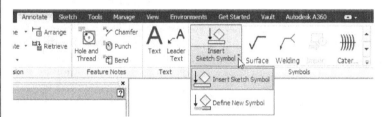

Figure 6–23

- Once a sketched symbol is saved to the drawing, you can also explicitly save it to a Symbol Library. The new Symbol Library is a drawing file used to store and provide easy access to symbols. Multiple libraries can be created. By saving a custom sketched symbol to a library drawing, you do not need to store the symbols in templates, or copy and paste them between drawings.

How To: Save to the Symbol Library

1. In the Drawing Resources dialog box, in the Sketch Symbols node, right-click on the symbol and select **Save to Symbol Library**. To save all symbols in the Sketch Symbols node, right-click the node and select **Save All to Symbol Library**. The Save to Symbol Library dialog box opens as shown in Figure 6–24.

The Save to Symbol Library dialog box always references the symbol library drawing file that have been created. This list is only empty the first time you access the command and create a library.

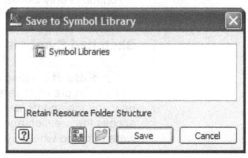

Figure 6–24

2. In the Save to Symbol Library dialog box, select an existing library from the list, or click (Create a new Library) to create a new library in the list.

3. (Optional) Click (Create a new folder) to create a new folder in the selected library to organize the symbols.

4. Click **Save**. The Symbol Library is stored in the Design Data directory on your system by default, and supports both .IDW and .DWG libraries. The symbol library locations can be customized on the *File* tab of the Application Options.

• To place a symbol (either from a library or locally stored in the drawing's Drawing Resources), click **Insert Sketched Symbol** in the Symbol panel. Alternatively, you can use the right-click **Insert** option that was previously available from the Drawing Resource folder. In either situation, the Sketch Symbols dialog box displays similar to that shown in Figure 6–25.

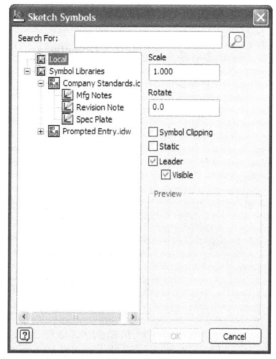

Figure 6–25

When using the new Sketch Symbols dialog box to insert a symbol, consider the following:

- The symbols shown in the dialog box will vary depending on:
  - The libraries you have created.
  - If there are local sketched symbols in the Drawing Resources folder of the current folder.

- Use the *Search For* field at the top of the dialog box to search for symbols stored in library drawings. Once results are found, the list is filtered to only display the symbols that match the search criteria.

- Select a symbol in the Local or Symbol Library lists to preview it prior to placement.

- If a symbol is placed from a library, the symbol is copied to the local drawing. To update symbols that might have changed, re-insert the symbol from the library drawing and in the Paste Resource dialog box select whether to replace the symbol or create a new one.

Practice 6a

Drawing Enhancements

Practice Objectives

- Create a new drawing file directly from an assembly file.
- Use the new Drawing View dialog box to create and orient views in a drawing.
- Create a Parts List for a displayed Design View Representation.
- Set components in a view as Transparent.
- Create a partial section view and customize how the cut line displays.
- Create a new symbol, save it to the Symbol Library, and place it in the drawing.

In this practice, you will create a new drawing file directly from the assembly environment and will place views. You will also add a parts list, additional views, and work with the new symbol library functionality in the drawing.

Task 1 - Create a new drawing file directly from an assembly model.

1. In the *Engine* folder, open **Radial Engine Final.iam**.

2. Right-click the model name at the top of the Model Browser and select **Create Drawing View**, as shown in Figure 6–26.

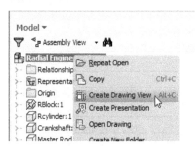

Figure 6–26

3. The Drawing Template dialog box opens, enabling you to define the template for the new drawing. Select the **ANSI (in).idw** template and then click **OK**.

4. The new Drawing View dialog box opens, indicating that the assembly is the active drawing model. A preview of the view displays on the drawing sheet.

5. Enter **.25** as the *Scale* value.

6. Place the cursor in the previewed Base view. and reposition the view so that it is fully displayed on the sheet.

7. Select and drag one of the four green manipulators on the corners of the previewed Base view to dynamically scale the view. Return the scale to **.1** using the Drawing View dialog box.

8. To create a user-defined orientation, click ⬇ on the ViewCube and select **Custom View Orientation**. The controls for defining the custom view orientation are the same as those in previous versions of the Autodesk Inventor software. Select **Finish Custom View** to complete the orientation without making a change.

9. Select **Front** on the ViewCube to reorient that Base view. You can select any face, edge, or corner on the ViewCube to reorient the view.

10. Select the small arrow at the center of the right-hand edge of the view boundary to create a projected view at a set distance from the Base view.

11. Select ✕ on a placed projected view to delete it from the drawing before the views have been finalized.

12. Alternatively, you can drag off the Base view to place a Projected view. Drag a projected view to the right of the Base view and place it by selecting the left mouse button.

13. Drag an isometric view to the top right-hand corner and place it.

14. Hover the mouse over the ViewCube associated with the Base view. Select 🏠 to reorient the Base view to its default isometric view. Note how all of the views update with the change.

15. Select ✕ on both the projected views to delete them.

16. Scale the Base view to **.25** and use the ViewCube to reorient the model, as shown in Figure 6–27.

Figure 6–27

17. Click **OK** to complete Base view creation.

18. Save the drawing as **Radial Engine Final.idw** in the *Engine* folder.

Task 2 - Create a Parts List.

---

1. Select the *Annotate* tab>Table panel and click (Parts List).

2. Select the view of the engine. In the Parts List dialog box, click **OK**.

3. Place the Parts List anywhere on the sheet. The Parts List is created as shown in Figure 6–28. All of the components in the drawing view display in the Parts List.

PARTS LIST			
ITEM	QTY	PART NUMBER	DESCRIPTION
1	1	RBlock	
2	5	Rcylinder	
3	1	Crankshaft	
4	1	Master Rod1	
5	5	PistonHeadPin	
6	5	Piston head	
7	1	Hub	
8	1	Shuttle	
9	3	Pro_blade	
10	3	Prop_Conrod	
11	4	Connector Arm1	

Figure 6–28

4. Double-click on the Base view to edit it.

5. In the Drawing View dialog box, select **No Prop** from the View drop-down list, as shown in Figure 6–29. This changes the view to display a view representation that was setup in the model and removes all the props and connecting rods from display.

Figure 6–29

6. Click **OK**. Note that the view updates; however, the parts list still shows the props and connecting rods as items in the table.

7. Right-click on the Parts List and select **Edit Parts List**.

8. To enable Inventor to take into account the design view used to create the view, click ⬒ (Filter Settings).

9. In the Filter Settings dialog box, set the following options, as shown in Figure 6–30.

- In the *Define Filter Item* area, select **Assembly View Representation** in the drop-down list.
- Select **No Prop** as the View Representation to be used.
- Select **Limit QTY to visible components only**.

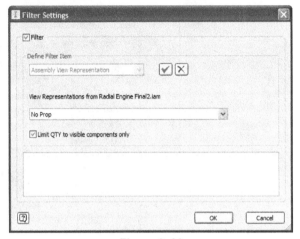

Figure 6–30

10. Click **OK** to assign the filter. Then, click **OK** a second time to close the Filter Settings dialog box.

11. Note that the Parts list updates and the props and connecting rods are no longer listed, as shown in Figure 6–31. Click **OK**. The parts list table also updates.

PARTS LIST			
ITEM	QTY	PART NUMBER	DESCRIPTION
1	1	RBlock	
2	5	Rcylinder	
3	1	Crankshaft	
4	1	Master Rod1	
5	5	PistonHeadPin	
6	5	Piston head	
7	1	Hub	
8	1	Shuttle	
11	4	Connector Arm1	

Figure 6–31

Task 3 - Create a second sheet and add views.

1. Add a second sheet to the drawing.

2. Add a Base view with the following specifics (as shown in Figure 6–32):

   - Use the **Master** View Representation.
   - Select **Front** as the view orientation.
   - Enter a **.15** *Scale* value.
   - Create three projected views by dragging to the right, left, and top right-hand corner of the Base view.
   - Set the view display as **Hidden Line Removed**.
   - Edit the isometric projection and set it as shaded.

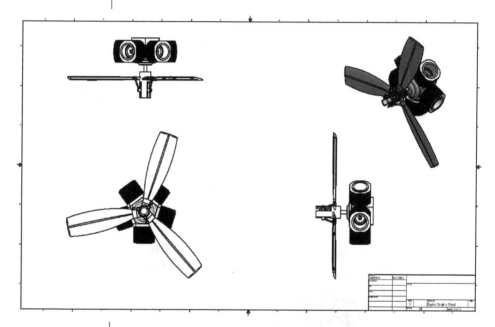

Figure 6–32

3. Expand the Model Browser node for the Base view so that all of the components of the assembly are listed.

4. Hold <Ctrl> and select the three **Pro_blade** (propeller blade) components in the assembly list. Right-click and select **Transparent**. The components update (as shown on the right in Figure 6–33) and are transparent so that the cylinders can be more easily seen.

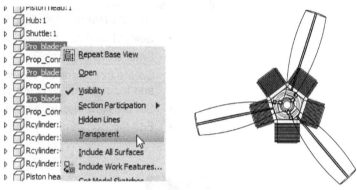

Figure 6–33

Task 4 - Create a Partial Section View.

1. Create the section view shown in Figure 6–34 using the top projected view as the reference view.

   - Create the cut line so that it snaps to the center of the Hub component and only partially cuts though the entire model.
   - In the *Cut Edges* area, select ⬙ (Set Cut Edges as Smooth).
   - Leave all the other defaults.
   - Click **OK** and place the view.

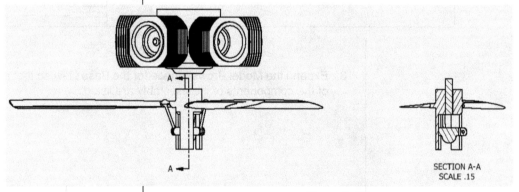

Figure 6–34

2. It is now possible with partial section views to customize the cut line to be jagged. Right-click on the section view and select **Edit Section Properties**.

3. In the Edit Section Properties dialog box, select ⬚ (Set Cut Edges as Jagged). Note how the cut edge of the view changes, as shown in Figure 6–35

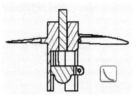 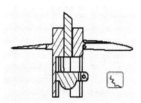

Cut Edge displayed as Smooth.   *Cut Edge displayed as Jagged.*

Figure 6–35

4. Return the cut edge to ⬚ (Set Cut Edges as Smooth) and complete the edit.

Task 5 - Create a custom symbol and save it to the library.

---

1. Select the *Annotate* tab. In the Symbol panel, click **Define New Symbol**. The command might be compressed in the **Insert Sketch Symbol** command, if not listed directly on the panel.

2. In the Create panel, click **A** (Text) and select a location to begin symbol creation. This symbol will only be text based.

3. Set **.24 in** as the font size, and enter the text shown in Figure 6–36. Use the **Bullet** text tool, as required. Click **OK**.

4. In the Insert panel, click ⬚ (Image) and select a location next to the text, similar to that shown in Figure 6–36. Select **Caution.png** from the *Engine* folder when prompted to select the image. Relocate the image as required.

⚠ During Assembly:
- Apply sparing amount of Blue Loctite.
- Torque fasteners to recommended value using torque wrench.
- Remove any excess Loctite.

Figure 6–36

*Your initials have been
included to create a
unique symbol in the
library. This is required if
this practice is
completed multiple
times on the same
computer.*

*The Save to Symbol
Library dialog box
always references the
symbol library drawing
files that have been
created. This list is only
empty the first time you
access the command
and create a library.*

5. Click **Finish Sketch** to complete the sketch.

6. Enter **Blue Loctite - <your initials>** as the name of the symbol and click **Save**.

7. In the *Drawing Resources* folder, right-click on the symbol in the **Sketch Symbols** node, and select **Save to Symbol Library**. The Save to Symbol Library dialog box opens, similar to that shown in Figure 6–37. It might vary if any libraries have already been created on this system.

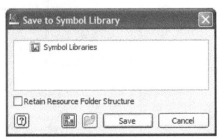

Figure 6–37

8. In the Save to Symbol Library dialog box, click (Create a new Library) to create a new library in the list. Enter **Assembly Instructions** as the name of the new library. If this library already exists, select it.

9. Click **Save**. The Symbol Library (**Assembly Instructions.idw**) is stored in the *Design Data* directory on your system and now contains the new symbol.

10. In the *Drawing Resources* folder, right-click on the symbol in the **Sketch Symbols** node and select **Delete**. This symbol is removed from the drawing. In the next task, you will add it back into the drawing from the library to simulate working with the symbol library.

Task 6 - Add the custom symbol to the drawing.

---

1. Select the *Annotate* tab. In the Symbol panel, click **Insert Sketch Symbol**. The command might be compressed in the **Define New Symbol** command because it is the command that was previously used.

2. Expand the **Assembly Instructions.idw** library, as shown in Figure 6–38. Note that the new symbol is listed in the library. Also, there are no symbols in the current drawing, as shown by the empty Local folder.

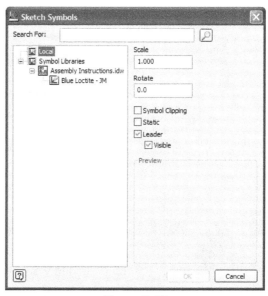

Figure 6–38

3. Select **Blue Loctite - *<your initials>***. The symbol displays in the new preview area in the Sketch Symbols dialog box. Maintain all of the default settings and click **OK**.

4. Place the symbol in the drawing, similar to that shown in Figure 6–39. To create the symbol without a leader, right click and select **Continue**.

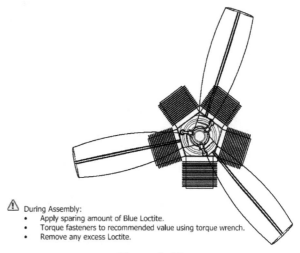

⚠ During Assembly:
- Apply sparing amount of Blue Loctite.
- Torque fasteners to recommended value using torque wrench.
- Remove any excess Loctite.

Figure 6–39

5. Save the drawing and close all the files.

Chapter Review Questions

1. An assembly drawing can be created directly from an assembly model; however, to create a drawing of a part model, you must first create the drawing and then assign the part model that will be documented.

   a. True

   b. False

2. Which of the following enables you to create a custom view orientation for the first Base view in a drawing? (Select all that apply.)

   a. Drawing View dialog box>*Component* tab

   b. Drawing View dialog box>*Display Options* tab

   c. Extended ViewCube options for the Base view

   d. Reorient an assembly model and create the drawing from that environment to create the Base view.

3. The **Transparent** command enables you to remove a component from the display in a drawing view.

   a. True

   b. False

4. The new Initial View Scale drawing property is located in which of the following drawing property categories?

   a. Properties - Drawing

   b. Drawing Properties

   c. Sheet Properties

   d. Properties - Model

5. When creating a parts list that references a Design View (with components removed from the display), how can you ensure that the list of components in the parts list match the view?

   a. This is done automatically. The parts list always matches the view.

   b. Use the parts list filter settings.

   c. Use the parts list Column Chooser options.

   d. This is not possible.

6. Which of the following are valid alignment options for balloons? (Select all that apply.)

   e. Horizontal

   f. Vertical

   g. To View Boundary

   h. To Edge

7. Which of the following settings can be used prior to placing a leadered text annotation to specify only a single line segment is required?

   a. **Single leader**

   b. **Single-segment leader**

   c. **Single segment**

   d. This is not possible. You must right-click and select **Continue** to end the placement of leaders.

8. Which of the following are valid statements about custom sketched symbols? (Select all that apply.)

   a. Once a custom sketched symbol is created in a drawing it is automatically saved to the symbol library.

   b. Library files types include both .IDW and .DWG files.

   c. Library files are stored in the project files working directory.

   d. When inserting a custom symbol from a library you can use search tools to help refine the list of symbols that are available for selection.

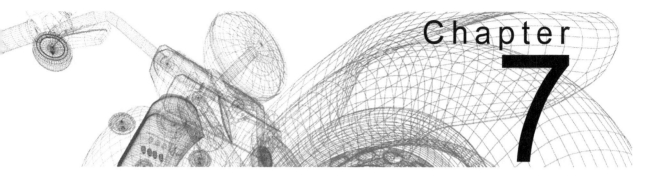

Chapter 7

Working with Imported Data

In this chapter, you will learn about the enhancements that have been incorporated into the Autodesk® Inventor® 2016 and 2017 software to ease the use of working with imported data. You will learn about the new Import dialog box and how it can be used to convert selected source data into an Inventor format, or use the reference option to maintain an associative link to the source CAD file. To complete the chapter, you will also lean how to work with associative AutoCAD® DWG files and how they can be used to create solid geometry in Autodesk Inventor.

Learning Objectives in this Chapter

- Import CAD data into the Autodesk Inventor software.
- Use an AutoCAD DWG file in an Autodesk Inventor part file so that the created geometry remains associative with the AutoCAD DWG file.

7.1 Importing CAD Data

File Import Types

Using the Autodesk Inventor 2017 software, you can import the file formats shown in Figure 7–1.

Figure 7–1

Importing Files

As of 2016, the Import dialog box has been enhanced to simplify the workflow.

How To: Import Data

1. In the **File** menu or Quick Access Toolbar, select **Open**. The Open dialog box displays.
2. In the Files of type drop-down list, select the file format that is to be imported.
3. Select the file to import and click **Open**. The Import dialog box opens.

Hint: Importing into an Existing File

You can import CAD Data into existing files using the following options:

- In an open part file, in the *3D Model* tab>Create panel, click

  🔲 (Import). The **Import** command is also available on the *Manage* tab>Import panel.

- In an assembly file, in the *Assemble* tab>expanded **Place**

  commands, click 🔲 (Place Imported CAD Files).

- If a part file is imported, a new Autodesk Inventor part file is created.

The imported geometries can be converted or referenced.

- If an assembly is imported, a new Autodesk Inventor assembly is created.
- The available options in the dialog box vary depending on the file format that is being imported.

In the example shown in Figure 7–2, a CATIA part file and an .IGS file were selected, as indicated by the filenames at the top of the dialog boxes.

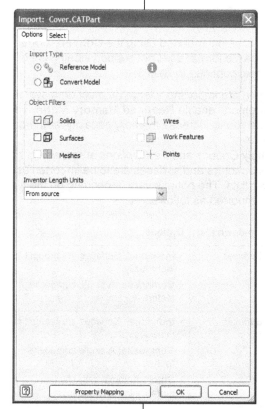 

Figure 7–2

4. In the *Import Type* area, select how the data will be imported:

With the release of 2017, Step files can now be imported by reference.

- Select **Reference Model** to import the data so that a reference is maintained to the source file. If this option is used, when changes are made to the source file, you can update the model in Autodesk Inventor to reflect the changes.
- Select **Convert Model** to import the geometry and break the link with the original model.

5. In the *Object Filters* area, select the data type to import (i.e., Solids, Surfaces, Meshes, Wires, Work Features, or Points).

6. In the *Inventor Length Units* area, specify the type of length unit to use for the imported geometry. The options enable you to maintain the same units as the data being imported (**From source**), or select from a list of standard units (e.g., inch, foot, millimeter, meter, etc).

7. Depending on the *Import Type,* proceed as follows:

   • If the data is being imported using the **Reference Model** option, there are no additional options that are available. Continue to Step 11.

   • If the data is being imported using the **Convert Model** option or the file format does not support it being imported by reference, continue to Step 8.

8. (Optional) If you are importing a large data set on a system with limited memory, enable **Reduced Memory Mode**. This option enables you to increase memory capacity, at the cost of performance.

9. In the *Assembly Options* and *Part Options* areas, select how the assembly structure and surfaces are to be imported using the drop-down lists. The options vary depending on the file format being imported as follows:

File Format	Drop-down List	Options
Parts	• Surfaces	• **Individual:** Surfaces are brought in individually. • **Composite:** A single composite feature.
IGES or STEP files	• Surfaces	• **Individual:** Surfaces are brought in individually. • **Composite:** A single composite feature. • **Stitch:** Automatically stitches surfaces together on import.
Assemblies	• Structure • Surfaces	• **Assembly:** The original assembly structure is maintained. • **Multi-body part:** Each component is imported as individual solid bodies in a single part. • **Composite Part:** Each part in an assembly is a composite. • The Part surface options that are available for assemblies are the same as those available for parts.

10. By default, the name of the newly created file that contains the imported geometry is the same as the imported filename. In the *File Names* area, enter a prefix or suffix to append to the default name in the *Name* field. Additionally, you can browse to a new directory or accept the default file location for the new file.

11. In the *Select* tab, click **Load Model** to add all of the model data to the dialog box and display a preview of the model in the graphics window.

12. (Optional) Click the circular node associated with each node to toggle its inclusion. By default, all nodes are included ().

The ability to map properties was introduced in Inventor 2017 (R2).

When the node displays, the geometry is excluded. To toggle multiple surfaces, select them and use the appropriate Status symbol at the top of the Import dialog box.

- Whether or not you can include or exclude geometry depends on the type of part or assembly that is being imported.

13. (Optional) Use the Property Mapping option at the bottom of the Import dialog box to map properties from the source file to Inventor properties. This is available for CATIA, SOLIDWORKS, NX, STEP, and Pro-ENGINEER/Creo file formats.

14. Once the options are set, click **OK** to open the imported solid in the Autodesk Inventor software.

Hint: Additional Information on Importing CAD Formats

For more details on the specific formats and versions of other CAD software products that are supported for import, search the Autodesk Inventor Help for "To Import Files from other CAD Systems" or "About Importing Files from other CAD Systems".

Hint: Overriding Properties

As of 2017, you can now specify property overrides for CATIA, SOLIDWORKS, NX, STEP, and Pro-ENGINEER/Creo if the file has been imported as a reference file. To override, right-click on the file in the Model Browser and select **iProperties**. In the iProperties dialog box you can override properties in the *Summary*, *Project*, *Status*, or *Custom* tabs. Once overwritten, they display in blue. To return them to their default value, right-click on the *Value* field and select **Value From Source**.

Hint: Importing IGS File Data

When importing an .IGS file, you can select the specific surfaces to import on the *Select* tab, as shown in Figure 7–3.

Figure 7–3

How To: Include or Exclude Surfaces

1. Select the *Select* tab.
2. Select **Load Model** to add all of the model data to the dialog box and display a preview of the model in the graphics window.
3. Click the circular node associated with each surface to toggle its inclusion. By default, all surfaces are included

    (⊕). When the ⊖ node displays, the surface is excluded. To toggle multiple surfaces, select them and use the appropriate Status symbol at the top of the Import dialog box.

7.2 Associative DWG Files

Previously, when an AutoCAD .DWG file was selected for opening in the Autodesk Inventor software, you could either open the file directly or import it so that it is converted into an Autodesk Inventor DWG file. These two options represented two of the methods that could be used to view and use AutoCAD DWG files in the Autodesk Inventor software.

As of 2016, you can now also import an AutoCAD DWG file into an Autodesk Inventor part file as an associative underlay. The DWG underlay can be imported on one or more work planes or faces, enabling you to project it into sketches and use it to create associative geometry. If changes are made in the source AutoCAD DWG file, the change can be updated in the Autodesk Inventor file. Additionally, in assembly files, you can use constraints and joints to create relationships between a DWG underlay geometry and a part.

Importing a DWG File as an Underlay

How To: Import an Autodesk DWG File as an Associative Underlay

1. Start a new part file using a template and save the file. A DWG file cannot be imported into a new, unsaved file.

2. In the *3D Model* tab>Create panel, click ⬚ (Import). Select and open an AutoCAD DWG file.

3. Select an origin plane or planar face to import the DWG file onto.

4. Select a origin point reference to locate the DWG file.

5. Click **OK** when prompted that inserting an AutoCAD DWG produces an associative underlay. The DWG file is listed in the Model Browser as an independent node.

- To redefine the placement plane and origin point used to locate the file, right-click on the filename and select **Redefine**, as shown in Figure 7–4. You are then prompted to select a new plane and origin point to locate the file.

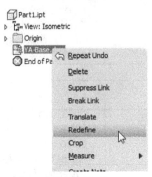

Figure 7–4

Controlling Layer Visibility

Once a DWG file has been imported as an underlay, you can control its layer visibility.

How To: Control the Layer Visibility

1. Right-click on the DWG file in the Model Browser and select **Layer Visibility**. The Layer Visibility dialog box opens, as shown in Figure 7–5.

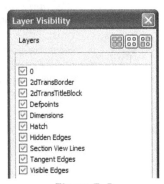

Figure 7–5

2. Toggle on/off the layer names to customize the data that will be imported.
   - Use the filter settings at the top of the dialog box to quickly clear, select all, or invert the selected layers.
   - The visibility of any of the layers can be controlled at any time using this dialog box.
3. Click **OK** to close the Layer Visibility dialog box.

Moving an Underlay

If the imported file does not display in the correct location relative to the model's origin, it can be translated.

How To: Move a DWG Underlay

1. Right-click on the DWG file in the Model Browser and select **Translate**. A translation triad displays on the selected origin point.
2. Using the mini-toolbar, move the AutoCAD DWG file relative to the model's origin, as required:
   - In the mini-toolbar, click **Locate** and select a new reference on the imported DWG file to reposition the triad.
   - In the mini-toolbar, click **Snap To** and select the Origin Center Point or another point to align the DWG underlay as required in the model.

3. Click to complete the translation.

Cropping an Underlay

An imported DWG underlay can be cropped to simplify the amount of detail that displays. Cropping can also help improve performance.

How To: Crop Entities in a DWG Underlay

1. Right-click on the DWG file in the Model Browser and select **Crop**.
2. In the graphics window, drag a bounding box around the entities that you want to keep.
3. Right-click in the graphics window and select **OK (Enter)** to complete the crop. Any geometry that was not included in the selected area is automatically removed.

- Once an DWG underlay file is cropped, a **Crop** node is added to the Model Browser.

- Only one crop can be made to a file, thus if a change is required, you must delete the crop element and read it. To delete a Crop, right-click on the element in the Model Browser and select **Delete**.

Using an Underlay to Create Geometry

To use the imported underlay to create solid geometry that remains associative to the AutoCAD DWG file, consider the following along with your standard sketching and feature creation techniques:

*   Start the creation of a new sketch. In the *Sketch* tab>Create panel, expand the Project Geometry options and select

    (Project DWG Geometry). By projecting the DWG geometry you can maintain the reference between the sketch and the DWG file. Use the filter options in the mini-toolbar to project single geometry ( ), connected geometry ( ), or a DWG Block ( ). Click ⊗ to close the mini-toolbar and cancel the Project DWG Geometry command.

*   When projected, all of the entities are fully constrained. Consider creating Driven Dimensions to identify key dimensions in the underlay that can be used to drive solid geometry. For the example shown in Figure 7–6, the Driven Dimension can now be used to define the depth of the model.

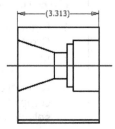

Figure 7–6

*   In the Model Browser, right-click on the imported DWG file to access the **Suppress Link** and **Break Link** options. These options can be used to either temporarily break the link with the source DWG file (**Suppress Link**) or permanently break the link (**Break Link**).

An imported AutoCAD DWG file can also be used as a layout reference to assemble components in an Inventor assembly file. For the example shown in Figure 7–7, the factory floor layout is an AutoCAD DWG file that can be used for assembly references in a top-level assembly.

- The underlay must be placed into an Inventor part file, which is then assembled as a component in the assembly.

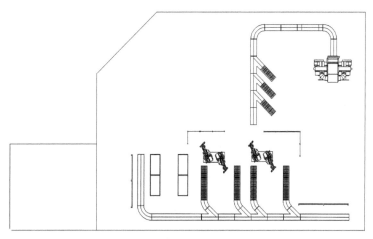

Figure 7–7

Hint: Associative DWG Underlays in Drawings

To include a DWG underlay in a drawing view, right-click on the Associative DWG file associated with the view and select **Include**, as shown in Figure 7–8. Once included, you can add text, dimensions, manage layers, or edit line types to appropriately annotate the underlay geometry.

Figure 7–8

Practice 7a

Opening a CATIA Assembly

Practice Objectives

- Open a CATIA assembly file in Autodesk Inventor by referencing the source data.
- Incorporate changes made to the CATIA model in the Autodesk Inventor model.

In this practice, you open a CATIA assembly file using the **Reference Model** option. By importing the CAD data in this way, changes made in the source model update in the Autodesk Inventor assembly. A change in a CATIA model is made, and you will update the change in the assembly. The final model is shown in Figure 7–9.

Figure 7–9

Task 1 - Import a CATIA assembly file in Autodesk Inventor.

1. In the Quick Access Toolbar, click .

2. In the Open dialog box, navigate to the *SparkPlug* folder in the practice files folder.

3. In the Files of type drop-down list, select **CATIA V5 Files**.

4. Select **SparkPlug.CATProduct** and click **Open**. The Import dialog box opens.

5. Select **Reference Model** from the *Import Type* area. This assembly is required for use in an Autodesk Inventor assembly model. If changes are made in the source model, the changes must be updated in the Inventor version of the file.

6. In the *Object Filters* area, ensure that only **Solids** is selected. Clear any other options.

*Alternatively, the CATIA assembly could be placed in an existing assembly using **Place Imported CAD Files** on the Component panel.*

7. In the *Inventor Length Units* area, ensure that **From source** is selected. The dialog box updates as shown in Figure 7–10.

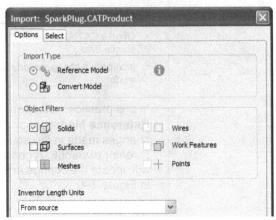

Figure 7–10

8. In the *Select* tab, click **Load Model**. A preview of the CATIA assembly displays in the graphics window and the components of the assembly are listed.

9. Click the circular ⊕ node associated with the **Wire.1** component to toggle its status to Excluded (⊖). Leave all of the other components as ⊕ Included.

10. Click **OK** to close the dialog box and import the geometry. The assembly is listed in the Model Browser, as shown in Figure 7–11.

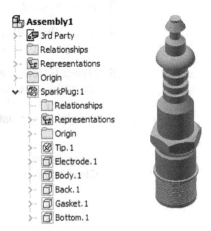

Figure 7–11

11. Save the assembly as **Sparkplug.iam** in the *SparkPlug* folder.

Task 2 - Edit the imported options.

1. In the Model Browser, right-click on **SparkPlug:1** and select **Edit Import** to open the Import dialog box that was used to import the files.

2. In the *Select* tab, select ⬤ adjacent to the **Wire.1** component to include it in the imported geometry.

3. Click **OK** to confirm the change. Note that the component is now listed in the Model Browser.

Task 3 - Edit the imported model geometry.

In this portion of the practice you will simulate making a design change in the original CATIA model. To do this you will rename a new file that has been provided to you so that it is used instead of the existing file. This new file has had modifications made to it in CATIA. By renaming, you are simulating that the change was made locally to the CATIA file.

1. In Windows Explorer, navigate to your practice files folder and open the *SparkPlug* folder.

2. Select the **Body.CATPart** file and rename it to **Body_OLD.CATPart**.

3. Select the **Body_UPDATED.CATPart** file and rename it to **Body.CATPart**.

4. Return to the Autodesk Inventor software.

5. Note in the Model Browser that the ⚡ icon displays next to the **SparkPlug:1** imported geometry node (it might take a moment to update). In the Quick Access Toolbar, click 🔲 (Local Update) to update the imported geometry with the change that was made in the source model. The model displays as shown in Figure 7–12.

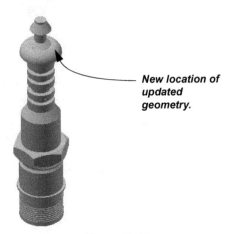

New location of updated geometry.

Figure 7–12

6. In Model Browser, right-click on **SparkPlug:1** and note the **Suppress Link** and **Break Link** options. These options can be used to either temporarily break the link with the source CATIA model (**Suppress Link**) or permanently break the link (**Break Link**).

7. Save the file and close the window.

Practice 7b

Import Associative DWG Data into a Part File

Practice Objective

- Open an AutoCAD DWG file directly into an Autodesk Inventor part file and work with the data.

In this practice, you will import an AutoCAD DWG file into an Autodesk Inventor file as an underlay. You will control the layer visibility and its location in the file so that the underlay can be used to project geometry onto sketches. The sketch geometry will then be used to create a 3D model. The geometry that will be created is shown in Figure 7–13.

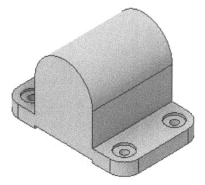

Figure 7–13

Task 1 - Create a new Autodesk Inventor model and import AutoCAD data.

1. Start a new part file using the **Standard (in).ipt** template.

2. Save the file as **AssociativeDWG.ipt**. A DWG file cannot be imported into a new, unsaved file.

3. In the *3D Model* tab>Create panel, click ⬚ (Import).

4. In the Import dialog box, expand the Files of type drop-down list and select **AutoCAD DWG Files (*.dwg)**.

5. Select **YA-Base.dwg** from the practice files folder and click **Open**.

6. Select the XY Origin plane as the plane to import the DWG file to.

7. Select the projected Origin Center Point as the centerpoint for the import.

8. Click **OK** when prompted that inserting an AutoCAD DWG produces an associative underlay.

9. Review the three 2D views. Note that the side view is a section view.

Task 2 - Set the Layer Visibility on the AutoCAD DWG file.

1. Right-click on **YA-Base.dwg** in the Model Browser and select **Layer Visibility**. The Layer Visibility dialog box opens.

2. In the filter settings at the top of the dialog box, click ⬚ (Clear All) to clear all the layers from being displayed.

3. Select **Hidden Edges**, **Tangent Edges**, and **Visible Edges**.

4. Click **OK** to close the Layer Visibility dialog box. The visibility of any of the layers can be controlled at any time using this dialog box.

Task 3 - Crop the AutoCAD DWG file.

1. Right-click on **YA-Base.dwg** in the Model Browser and select **Crop**.

2. Drag a bounding box around the two views shown in Figure 7–14. The box defines which entities in the underlay file will remain in the file.

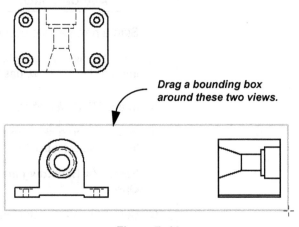

Drag a bounding box around these two views.

Figure 7–14

3. Right-click and select **OK (Enter)** to remove the entities outside the bounding box from view.

Task 4 - Translate the AutoCAD DWG file relative to the model's origin.

---

1. Expand the **Origin** node in the Model Browser and toggle on the visibility of the Center Point.

2. Using the Navigation Bar, select **Zoom All** to refit the model so that both the Origin Center Point and the drawing display on the screen. If you are using a white background you may have difficulty seeing the yellow origin center point.

3. Right-click on **YA-Base.dwg** in the Model Browser and select **Translate**.

4. A triad displays on the Origin Center Point. Click **Locate** in the mini-toolbar. Select the center point of the internal hole, as shown in Figure 7–15.

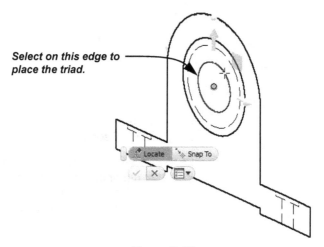

Select on this edge to place the triad.

Figure 7–15

5. Click ✓ to close the mini-toolbar and complete the translation.

6. Return the model to its Home View using the ViewCube.

Task 5 - Create associative geometry from the DWG file.

1. Create a new 2D sketch on the XY plane.

2. In the *Sketch* tab>Create panel, expand the Project Geometry options and select (Project DWG Geometry).

3. In the mini-toolbar, select (Project Connected Geometry) and select on an outside edge in the Front view, as shown on the left in Figure 7–16. All connected edges are projected. Project the outside loop or single edges on the section view, as shown on the right of Figure 7–16.

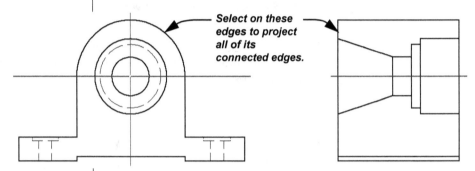

Select on these edges to project all of its connected edges.

Figure 7–16

4. Click ⊗ to close the mini-toolbar and cancel the Project DWG Geometry command.

5. Create a dimension in the side section view to define the depth of the model. Once placed, you will be prompted that the dimension will over-constrain the sketch. Click **Accept** to place the dimension as a Driven Dimension, as shown in Figure 7–17.

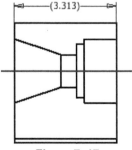

Figure 7–17

6. Finish the sketch.

7. Right-click in the graphics window and click **Dimension Display>Name** to display the name of the dimension value.

8. Create an Extrude and select the section shown in Figure 7–18. Enter **d0** (or name of your Driven Dimension) as the value for the extruded depth.

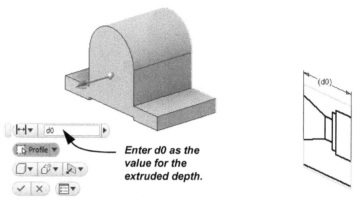

Enter d0 as the value for the extruded depth.

Figure 7–18

9. Complete the feature.

Task 6 - Insert the DWG on another plane and create additional geometry.

---

1. In the *3D Model* tab>Create panel, click (Import).

2. In the Import dialog box, select **YA-Base.dwg** from the practice files folder and click **Open**.

3. Select the plane and origin point shown in Figure 7–19 as the references to import the DWG file.

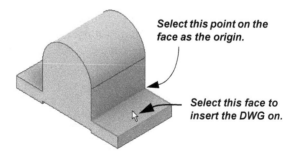

Select this point on the face as the origin.

Select this face to insert the DWG on.

Figure 7–19

---

4. When prompted that inserting an AutoCAD DWG produces an associative underlay, click **OK**.

5. Right-click on the newly imported **YA-Base.dwg** in the Model Browser and select **Layer Visibility**. The Layer Visibility dialog box opens. Note that the same visibility settings are set. Click **OK** to close the Layer Visibility dialog box.

6. In the Navigation Bar, select **Zoom All** to refit the model to see the solid geometry and the new underlay.

7. Right-click on newly imported **YA-Base.dwg** in the Model Browser and select **Translate**.

8. A triad displays, by default, on the point that was selected on the placement face. Click **Locate** in the mini-toolbar. Select the point shown in Figure 7–20 on the newly imported underlay.

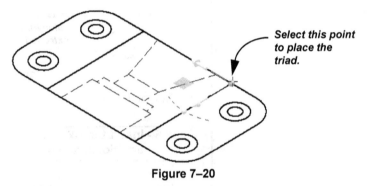

Select this point to place the triad.

Figure 7–20

9. Click ☑ to close the mini-toolbar and complete the translation.

10. Both underlays are on different planes and are visible. Right-click on the first **YA-Base.dwg** and clear the **Visibility** option. You can toggle the display of underlays on and off as required.

11. Create a new sketch on the same face that was used to place the latest DWG underlay file.

12. In the Create panel, click (Project DWG Geometry).

13. In the mini-toolbar, ensure that (Project Single Geometry) is selected and select the four arcs on the outside corners of the view shown in Figure 7–21 to project them.

14. Project one large and one small circle, as shown in Figure 7–21. Close the mini-toolbar or cancel the command.

15. Create the three Driven Dimensions shown in Figure 7–21.

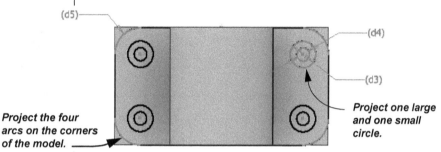

(d5)

(d4)

(d3)

Project the four arcs on the corners of the model.

Project one large and one small circle.

Figure 7–21

16. While in the same sketch, project the required edges and create the reference dimension shown in Figure 7–22.

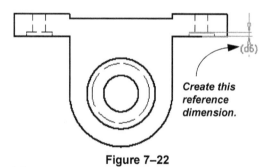

(d6)

Create this reference dimension.

Figure 7–22

17. Finish the sketch.

18. Create a Fillet.

The dimension name may vary depending on the order that you created the Driven Dimensions in the sketch.

19. Select the four vertical edges on the outside of the model. Enter **d5** (or name of your Driven Dimension) as the value of the fillet, as shown in Figure 7–23. This ensures the size of the fillet is driven by the projected geometry.

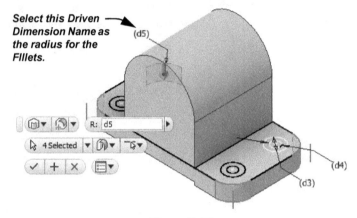

Select this Driven Dimension Name as the radius for the Fillets.

Figure 7–23

20. Complete the feature.

21. Create a Hole. Select **Concentric** as the placement type.

22. Change the hole type to **Counterbore** and select the placement plane and concentric references shown in Figure 7–24.

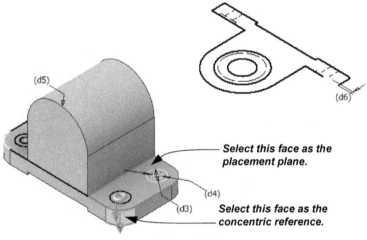

Select this face as the placement plane.

Select this face as the concentric reference.

Figure 7–24

23. Enter the dimension values for the hole using the Driven Dimensions that were created in the sketch, as shown in Figure 7–25. Ensure that you enter the correct dimension name to match the counterbore dimensions. Create the hole as **Through All**.

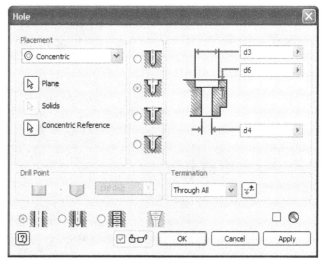

Figure 7–25

24. Complete the feature.

25. Create the additional three counterbore holes using the Concentric option and the same Driven Dimensions.

26. Toggle off the visibility of the second imported DWG underlay and the sketch. The model displays as shown in Figure 7–26.

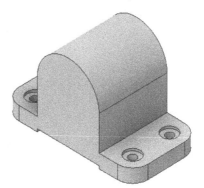

Figure 7–26

27. Save the file.

Task 7 - Replace the YA-Base.dwg with a modified version.

1. Open Windows Explorer and navigate to the practice files folder.

2. Rename **YA-Base.dwg** to **YA-Base_Original.dwg**.

3. Rename **YA-Base_Updated.dwg** to **YA-Base.dwg**. This new file has had changes made to the file to increase the size of the holes and the depth of the model.

4. Return to Autodesk Inventor and review the **AssociativeDWG.ipt**. The Model Browser indicates that **YA-Base.dwg** has been updated, as shown by the lightening bolt icons in Figure 7–27.

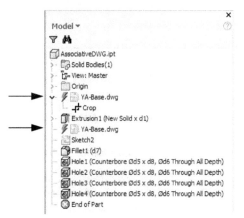

Figure 7–27

5. In the Quick Access toolbar, select ⬛ (Local Update). Note that the model updates as shown in Figure 7–28.

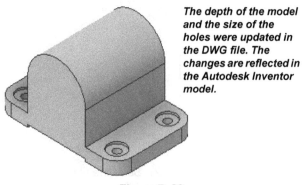

The depth of the model and the size of the holes were updated in the DWG file. The changes are reflected in the Autodesk Inventor model.

Figure 7–28

6. In the Model Browser, right-click on either of the **YA-Base.dwg** files and note the **Suppress Link** and **Break Link** options. These options can be used to either temporarily break the link with the source DWG file (**Suppress Link**) or permanently break the link (**Break Link**).

7. Save the model and close the window.

Task 8 - (Optional) Continue modeling the solid geometry.

After you have finished creating all of the practices in this chapter, continue to add the geometry from the DWG file into the Autodesk Inventor model. The only remaining feature is a revolved cut. To create this, consider creating a workplane and project the section that is to be revolved. Alternatively, edit one of the sketches and add more Driven Dimensions that can be used to drive additional hole features.

Practice 7c | Associative DWG Layout

Practice Objectives

- Import an AutoCAD .DWG file as an underlay in an Autodesk Inventor part file.
- Assemble the underlay part file as the base grounded component and reference it to place and create components.

In this practice, you will begin by creating a new part file that imports an AutoCAD DWG file for use as an underlay. The underlay is imported so that associativity is maintained between the files. The part file is then used in an assembly to constrain and create new components in the assembly. To complete the practice, a change is made in the original DWG file and the updates are shown to reflect in the assembly file. The geometry that will be created is shown in Figure 7–29.

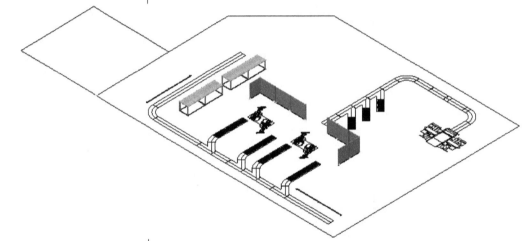

Figure 7–29

Task 1 - Create a new Autodesk Inventor model and import AutoCAD data.

1. Start a new part file using the **Standard (in).ipt** template.

2. A DWG file cannot be imported into a new, unsaved file. Save the new file as **FactoryLayout.ipt**.

3. In the *3D Model* tab>Create panel, click ⬚ (Import).

4. In the Import dialog box, expand the Files of type drop-down list and select **AutoCAD DWG Files (*.dwg)**.

5. Select **Layout Example.dwg** from the practice files folder and click **Open**.

6. Select the XZ Origin plane as the plane to import the DWG file.

7. Select the projected Origin Center Point as the centerpoint for the import.

8. Click **OK** when prompted that inserting an AutoCAD DWG produces an associative underlay.

9. Review the factory layout. The orientation of the drawing should be rotated 180 degrees and the origin point needs to be repositioned. In the next task you will reorient the imported DWG file.

Task 2 - Translate the AutoCAD DWG file relative to the model's origin.

---

1. Expand the **Origin** node in the Model Browser. Toggle on the visibility of the Center Point and note where it is located.

2. Right-click on **Layout Example.dwg** in the Model Browser and select **Translate**.

3. A triad displays on the Origin Center Point. Select the rotation handle shown in Figure 7–30 to enable the rotation of the imported DWG file.

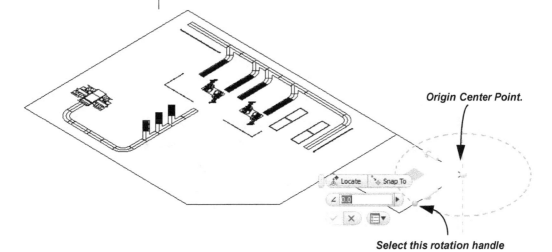

Origin Center Point.

Select this rotation handle (gray dot) to enable rotation.

Figure 7–30

---

4. Enter **180** to rotate the DWG file.

5. Click **Locate** in the mini-toolbar and select the point where the two rooms join, as shown in Figure 7–31.

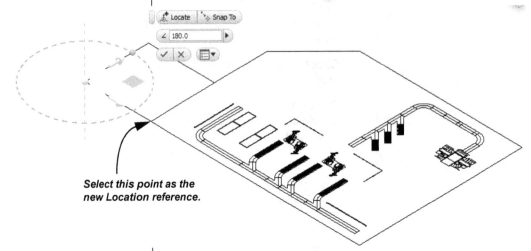

Select this point as the new Location reference.

Figure 7–31

6. Click **Snap To** in the mini-toolbar and select the Origin Center Point in the Model Browser to align the DWG underlay and the reference point on the drawing.

7. Click ✓ to close the mini-toolbar and complete the translation. The model should display as shown in Figure 7–32.

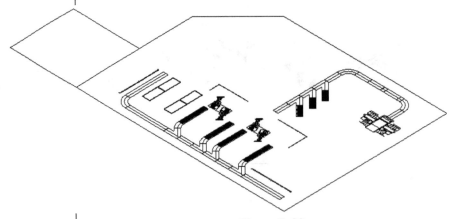

Figure 7–32

Task 3 - Set the Layer Visibility for the AutoCAD DWG file.

1. Right-click on **Layout Example.dwg** in the Model Browser and select **Layer Visibility**. The Layer Visibility dialog box opens. This dialog box enables you to control the DWG layers that display in the Autodesk Inventor model.

2. Select **Slab** in the list and note how additional entities are added to the view. As these are not required, you can leave this option cleared.

3. Select **Walls-Interior** to clear the option. Note how all of the entities are cleared. In this drawing all of the entities have been added to this layer. Select **Walls-Interior** again to enable the option.

4. Click **OK** to close the Layer Visibility dialog box. The visibility of layers can be controlled at any time using this dialog box.

5. Save the model.

Task 4 - Use the associative DWG file as a reference for assembling and creating components in an assembly.

1. Start a new assembly file using the **Standard (in).iam** template.

2. Place one instance of **FactoryLayout.ipt** into the assembly file. Right-click and select **Place Grounded at Origin** to assemble the part as the base model and ground it.

3. Press <Esc> to cancel the assembly of additional instances of the **FactoryLayout.ipt** file.

4. Place a single instance of **Table.iam** into the assembly file, as shown in Figure 7–33.

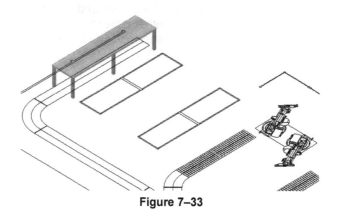

Figure 7–33

5. In the *Assembly* tab>Relationships panel, click

    (Constrain).

6. Using the Place Constraint dialog box, assign the following constraints to fully locate the table relative to the **FactoryLayout.ipt** file:

    - Mate the XZ plane of the table component to the XZ plane of the assembly. Use the **Flush** orientation.
    - Add two Mate constraints that align the edges of the table legs and the border of the table's layout in the X and Z directions, as shown in Figure 7–34.

Mate the front edge of the table leg with the edge of the table layout.

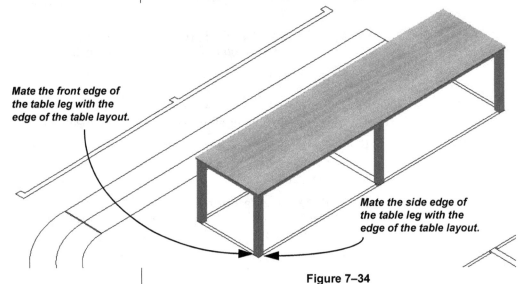

Mate the side edge of the table leg with the edge of the table layout.

Figure 7–34

7. Close the Place Constraints dialog box.

8. Place a second instance of **Table.iam** and constrain it to the other table layout. The final assembly should display as shown in Figure 7–35.

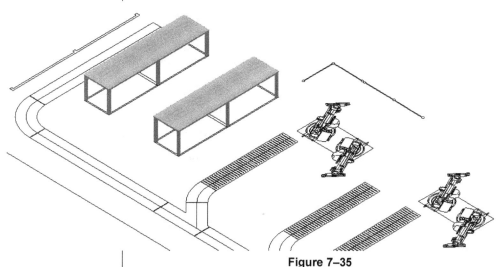

Figure 7–35

9. Save the file as **Factory.iam**.

___

Task 5 - Create part geometry using the AutoCAD DWG underlay as a reference.

___

1. In the *Assembly* tab>Component panel, click (Create) to start a new part file in the context of the assembly.

2. In the Create In-Place Component dialog box, enter **Screen.ipt** as the name of the new file and assign **Standard(in).ipt** as the part template to be used.

3. Select the XZ plane of the assembly as the sketch plane reference for the new part. **Screen.ipt** becomes the active component in the assembly (if not, activate it).

4. In the *3D Model* tab>Sketch panel, click (Start 2D Sketch).

5. Select the XY plane in the Screen model as the sketching plane for the sketch.

6. In the *Sketch* tab>Create panel, expand **Project Geometry** and select (Project DWG Geometry).

7. In the mini-toolbar, ensure that 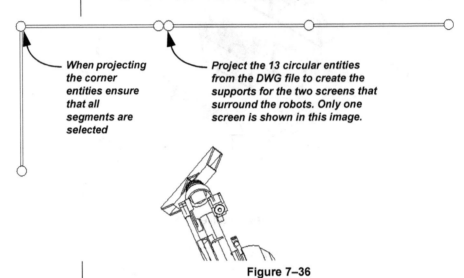 (Project Single Geometry) is selected. Select the 13 circular entities described in Figure 7–36. If the entire entity is not selected, it cannot be extruded in a later step.

When projecting the corner entities ensure that all segments are selected

Project the 13 circular entities from the DWG file to create the supports for the two screens that surround the robots. Only one screen is shown in this image.

Figure 7–36

8. Finish the sketch and rename the sketch as **Supports**.

9. Create a second sketch on the XY plane and start the (Project DWG Geometry) option.

10. In the mini-toolbar, select (Project Connected Geometry) and project the 9 rectangles that are used to define the screen geometry between the supports, as shown in Figure 7–37.

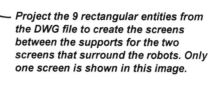

Project the 9 rectangular entities from the DWG file to create the screens between the supports for the two screens that surround the robots. Only one screen is shown in this image.

Figure 7–37

11. Finish the sketch and rename the sketch as **Screens**.

12. Use the **Extrude** command to create the screen geometry shown in Figure 7–38.

   - Extrude the 13 circular entities in the Supports sketch to a height of **72 in**.
   - Extrude the 9 rectangular entities in the Screens sketch to a height of **70 in**.

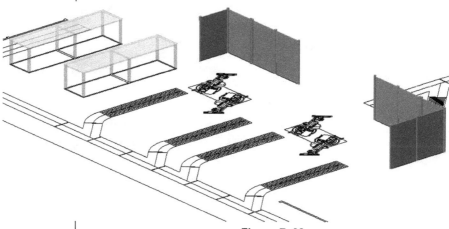

Figure 7–38

13. Reactivate the top-level assembly.

14. Save the assembly and the newly created part file.

Task 6 - Update the DWG underlay and the associated geometry.

1. Open Windows Explorer and navigate to the practice files folder.

2. Rename **Layout Example.dwg** to **Layout Example_OLD.dwg**.

3. Rename **Layout Example_Updated.dwg** to **Layout Example.dwg**. This new file has had changes made to the file to relocate the tables and change the size of one of the screens.

4. Return to Autodesk Inventor and note that the 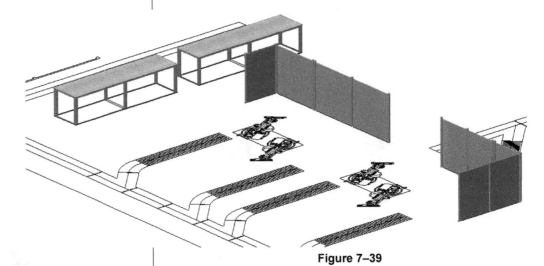 (Local Update) option is available in the Quick Access toolbar. Click (Local Update) to update the assembly, as shown in Figure 7–39.

Figure 7–39

5. Save the assembly and close the files.

Chapter Review Questions

1. Which of the following options is used to import data so that when changes are made in the source CAD file it can be updated in the Autodesk Inventor software?

   a. **Reference Model**

   b. **Convert Model**

2. Which of the following icons indicates that items are not being imported when set on the *Select* tab in the Import dialog box?

   a.

   b.

3. Which of the following are Direct Edit tools that are available in the Direct Edit mini-toolbar? (Select all that apply.)

   a. **Move**

   b. **Size**

   c. **Define Envelopes**

   d. **Rotate**

   e. **Remove Details**

   f. **Delete**

   g. **Scale**

4. The green dot that is highlighted on a face that is being relocated using the **Direct Edit** command indicates where the triad is placed.

   a. True

   b. False

5. Which of the following enables you to define the measurement reference point when using **Direct Edit**?

   a. **Measure From**

   b. **Snap To**

   c.

   d. **Snap Parallel**

6. Which of the following icons displays in the Direct Edit mini-toolbar when a face in the exterior geometry on the model is selected for deletion?

   a.

   b.

   c.

   d.

7. Which of the following are true statements regarding importing AutoCAD DWG data as an underlay into an Autodesk Inventor model? (Select all that apply.)

   a. The DWG data can only be imported onto a single plane in the model.

   b. The layers in the DWG underlay can be set to display only specific layers.

   c. The **Translate** command enables you to relocate the DWG underlay onto another plane.

   d. Use the **Project Geometry** command to project and use DWG data in a sketch.

   e. The DWG data that is imported remains unassociated with the source data.

   f. The visibility of the DWG underlays can be controlled using the **Visibility** option.

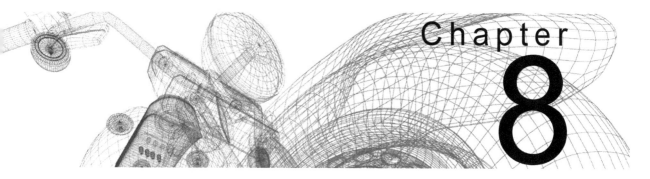

Chapter 8

Generative Shape Design

The Generative Shape Design tool introduced in the Autodesk® Inventor® 2017 software enables designers to set design criteria for a mass reduction target in a model. Based on assigned materials, constraints, and loads, the system returns a design suggestion that can be used to manipulate the model geometry to reduce its mass. Although this tool recommends a new shape, the manipulation is done manually using standard 3D modeling features. Once modified, stress analysis tools should be used on the model to ensure that it meets structural requirements This functionality was introduced in Inventor with the release of the 2016 (R2) software.

Learning Objectives in this Chapter

- Create a Shape Generator study that sets a goal to meet a mass reduction target.
- Assign criteria in a Shape Generator study to accurately define a model's working environment.
- Promote a Shape Generator study to the modeling environment.

8.1 Shape Generator

The Shape Generator tool in Autodesk Inventor enables you to design light-weight models based on specified requirements. First, you must start with an Inventor model that approximates the overall volume or shape that is required. After setting the requirements and running the Shape Generator, you are presented with a 3D mesh design that you can use as a guide to redesign your initial geometry. Figure 8–1 shows the progression of a model from its initial design, through Shape Generator, to the final design.

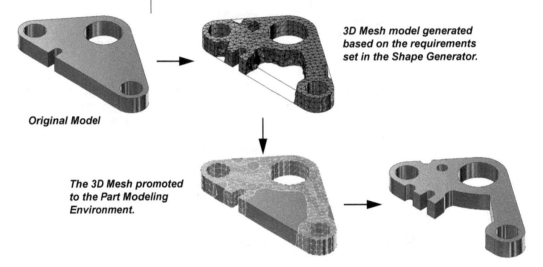

Original Model

3D Mesh model generated based on the requirements set in the Shape Generator.

The 3D Mesh promoted to the Part Modeling Environment.

Final Solid Geometry

Figure 8–1

How To: Generate a Design using Shape Generator

1. Open the model in the Shape Generator environment.
2. Define the material specification.
3. Apply constraints and loads that will represent the stresses that the part will encounter.
4. Define the Shape Generator Settings.
5. (Optional) Set zones that will be preserved during the analysis.
6. (Optional) Define symmetry in the model, if required.
7. Run the Shape Generator study.
8. Modify the initial design using the Shape Generator's 3D mesh as a guide for making modifications.

Preparing a Model for Shape Generator

Prior to initiating the Shape Generator tool, ensure that the Autodesk Inventor model represents the overall volume and shape of the intended geometry. The model should contain any required contact points (such as holes) that will represent pin locations and surfaces that will sustain forces.

Hint: Environment Support

Shape generator is only supported for single-body part modeling. It cannot be used for multi-body part or assembly design.

Opening Shape Generator

To open the Shape Generator environment, in the *3D Model* tab>Explore panel, click (Shape Generator). Click **OK** if prompted to review the learning tool. The *Analysis* tab opens as shown in Figure 8–2.

Figure 8–2

By default, a Shape Generator study is added to the Model Browser once the *Analysis* tab is opened. The commands on this tab enable you to do the following:

- Create multiple shape generator analyzes and manage them.

- Assign material to an analysis.

- Assign constraints and loads to an analysis to define how the model is loaded in its working environment.

- Set goals and criteria for the analysis. This involves defining regions in the model that should not be changed as well as symmetry planes. Additionally, you set the criteria against which the design will be optimized. For example, reduce weight by x% to achieve a specific weight.

- Generate the optimized shape.

- Export the 3D mesh of the optimized shape to the modeling environment.

To create additional Shape Generator studies, in the Manage panel, click  (Create Study), select **Shape Generator** in the Create New Study dialog box, and click **OK**.

> **Hint: Shape Generator in the Stress Analysis Environment**
>
> The Shape Generator functionality can also be accessed in the Stress Analysis environment. In the *3D Model* tab> Simulation panel, click (Stress Analysis). Once in the *Analysis* tab, click (Create Study), select **Shape Generator** in the Create New Study dialog box and click **OK**.

Material Assignment

In the Material panel, click (Assign) to open the Assign Materials dialog box, as shown in Figure 8–3.

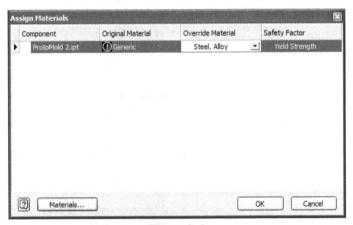

Figure 8–3

- Maintain the **(As Defined)** option in the Override Material drop-down list to run the generator using the original material that was set in the modeling environment.

- Select an alternate material type in the Override Material drop-down list to study an alternative material.

- Select **Materials** to open and use the Material browser to define materials.

- Set the Safety Factor based on the **Yield Strength** or the **Ultimate Tensile Strength**.

- The material information is stored in the **Material** node for the active study. Each study that is setup in the Shape Generator environment can use a unique material setting.

Applying Constraints

You can assign constraints to the model to accurately define the translational or rotational degrees of freedom that exist in its working environment. **Fixed**, **Pin**, and **Frictionless** constraints can be assigned.

How To: Add Constraints

1. In the *Analysis* tab>Constraints panel, select the type of constraint to be assigned. Alternatively, you can right-click on the **Constraints** node in the Model Browser and select the constraint type.

Constraint Type	Description
◥ᴵ **(Fixed)**	Rmoves all degrees of freedom on a face, edge, or vertex.
◯ **(Pin)**	When used with cylindrical surfaces, it prevents faces from moving or deforming in combinations of radial, axial, or tangential directions.
⬜ **(Frictionless)**	When used with flat or cylindrical surfaces, it prevents the surface from moving or deforming in the normal direction relative to the surface.

2. In the applicable Constraint dialog box, select ⬚ (Location) and select the location to which the constraint is being assigned. Select faces, edges, or vertices, as required.

3. Click ⬚ on the dialog box to access the additional constraint settings for each constraint type. The options in this portion of the dialog box enable you to further customize the constraint.

   - The **Display Glyph** option is used to enable/disable the visibility of the constraint glyph on the model.
   - A custom name can be assigned for the constraint, if required.
   - To apply a Fixed constraint with non-zero displacement, click **Use Vector Components** and enter X, Y, or Z values, as required.
   - For cylindrical surfaces, **Pin** constraints can be fixed radially, axially, or tangentially, as required. The default is to be fixed radially and axially.

4. Click **OK** to assign and close the dialog box. Alternatively, click **Apply** to assign the constraint and continue adding additional constraints of the same type.

Once added to the model, constraints are listed in the **Constraints** node in the Model Browser. To edit them, right-click on the constraint name and select **Edit <Constraint Type>**.

Applying Loads

To accurately determine a shape using shape generator, you can assign loads that represent the applied load on the model. **Force**, **Pressure**, **Bearing**, **Moment**, **Gravity**, **Remote Force**, and **Body** loads can be assigned.

How To: Add Loads

1. In the *Analysis* tab>Loads panel, select the type of load to be assigned. Alternatively, you can right-click on the **Loads** node in the Model Browser and select the load type.

Load Type	Description
(Force)	Assigns a force to a face, edge, or vertex. The force points to the inside of the part. You can assign the direction reference planar to a face or along a straight edge or axes.
(Pressure)	Assigns a pressure load to a face. Pressure is uniform and acts normal to the surface at all locations on the surface.
(Bearing)	Assigns a bearing load to a cylindrical face. By default, the load is along the axis of the cylinder and the direction of the load is radial.
(Moment)	Assigns a moment load to a face. You can assign the direction reference using a planar face, or along a straight edge or axes. The moment is applied around the direction to the selected face.
(Gravity)	Assigns the gravity load normal to the selected face or parallel with the selected edge.
(Remote Force)	Assigns a force at a specific point outside or inside the model. This option is located in the expanded Loads panel.
(Body)	Assign linear acceleration or angular velocity and acceleration for the model using a planar or cylindrical face as the input. This option is located on the expanded Loads panel.

You can only apply one Body load per Shape Generator study.

2. In the applicable Load dialog box, select [⬉] and select the reference to which the load is being assigned. Select faces, edges, or vertices, as required.

    *   A glyph displays on the model indicating the direction in which the load is applied. To change the direction, click

        [⬉] in the *Direction* area and select an alternate reference or flip the direction.

3. Define the magnitude of the load.

    *   Click [>>] for Force, Bearing, Moment, Gravity, Remote Force, and Body loads to assign the magnitude values using vector components.

4. Click [>>] on the dialog box to access additional settings for each load type. The options in this portion of the dialog box enable you to further customize the load.

    *   The **Display Glyph** option can be enabled/disabled to control the load glyph display, as required.
    *   The scale and color of the glyph display can be modified.
    *   A custom name can be assigned for the load, if required.

5. Click **OK** to assign and close the dialog box. Alternatively, click **Apply** to assign the load and continue adding additional loads of the same type.

Once loads are added to the model they are listed in the **Loads** node in the Model Browser. To edit them, right-click on the constraint name and select **Edit <Force Load>**.

> **Hint: Multiple Loads on a Face**
>
> Consider using the **Split** command to split a single face if the face experiences multiple loading situations.

Shape Generator Settings

The Shape Generator settings enable you to define the design criteria. To open the Shape Generator Settings dialog box (shown in Figure 8–4) click 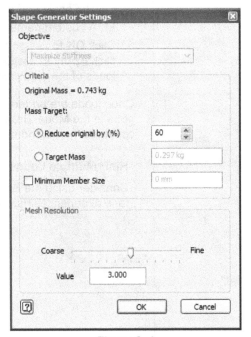 (Shape Generator Settings). By default, the 3D mesh model will be generated to maximize stiffness; however, you can also define the following additional criteria:

- Reduce the mass by a specified percentage or reduce it to a specific value.

- Define a specific member size that must be maintained during 3D mesh creation. This helps ensure that the mesh does not generate a wall thicknesses that can not be manufactured or might fail structural testing.

- The *Mesh Resolution* area provides a slider and a *Value* field that can be used to set the mesh resolution. A finer setting results in a smoother, higher quality mesh; however, it requires increased run time.

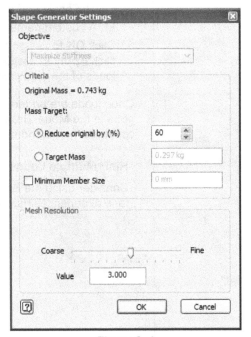

Figure 8–4

Preserving Regions

In most models, there will be regions of the design that should not be removed when generating a suggested 3D mesh. For example, specific areas around bolt holes or other supporting features may need to be maintained so that the model can function as required.

How To: Preserve an Area on the Model

1. In the Goals and Criteria panel, click (Preserve Region).

2. In the Preserve Region dialog box, click and select a face on the model. Based on the selection of the face, a default preserved region boundary will display on the model.

    *   If a planar face is selected, a bounding box displays around the face, as shown in Figure 8–5.

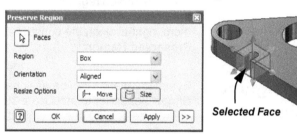

Figure 8–5

    *   If a cylindrical face is selected, a bounding cylinder displays around the face, as shown in Figure 8–6.

Figure 8–6

    *   If the assumption of **Box** or **Cylinder** is not correct, you can switch the option in the *Region* drop-down list.

3. Refine the location and size of the bounding shape.
   - Select **Move** and drag the center point of the displayed triad to reposition the bounding shape on the model.
   - Select **Size** and activate and drag any of the handles that radiate from the bounding shape.
   - Click ⊳⊳ to enter specific values for the center point and the bounding shape dimensions.
4. (Optional) In the expanded portion of the dialog box (⊳⊳) you can modify the glyph color, control its visibility, or enter a custom name for the preserved region.
5. Click **OK** to create the preserved region. Alternatively, click **Apply** to create the region and continue creating additional regions.

Once preserved regions are added to the model they are listed in the **Preserved Regions** node in the Model Browser. To edit them, right-click on the constraint name and select **Edit Preserved Region**.

Assigning Symmetry

Symmetry planes can be assigned in the model to force the Shape Generator to produce a 3D mesh result that is symmetric about a selected plane or up to three planes (XY, XZ, or YZ).

How To: Assign Symmetry

1. In the Goals and Criteria panel, click ▨ (Symmetry Plane).
2. By default, the symmetry planes are placed at the center of mass and are aligned with the global coordinate system. If required, use any of the following to modify the location of the default symmetry planes:
   - To align the symmetry plane with a local UCS, click

     ▱ (Local UCS) and select an active UCS. The symmetry plane is created in the local XY plane of the UCS.

   - To place at the center of mass, click ◉ (Center of mass). The UCS and symmetry plane are placed at the center of mass of the part.
   - To place at the center of the bounding box of the part,

     click ⊹ (Center of bounding box). The UCS and symmetry plane are placed at the center of bounding box of the part.

3. Toggle the active planes (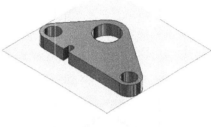), as required, to define the model symmetry. Active planes display red in the model.

4. (Optional) Click $\boxed{>>}$ to toggle the display of the symmetry glyph and assign a name for symmetry definition.

5. Click **OK** to close the dialog box. The symmetry Plane dialog box and a single symmetry plane are shown in Figure 8–7.

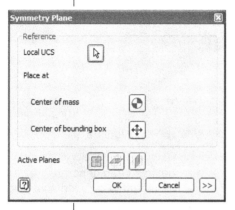

Figure 8–7

Once symmetry planes are added to the model, they are listed in the **Symmetry Planes** node in the Model Browser. To edit them, right-click on the constraint name and select **Edit Symmetry Plane**.

Run the Shape Generator

The expandable area at the bottom of the dialog box reports warnings or errors while the process is being run.

Once the analysis has been setup, click 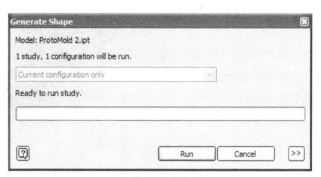 (Generate Shape) to open the Generate Shape dialog box, as shown in Figure 8–8. Click **Run** to start the shape generator.

Figure 8–8

Once shape generation is complete, you are presented with a recommended 3D mesh model that can be used to guide your model design. Figure 8–9 shows the original model and a resultant mesh model after constraints, loads, and criteria were set.

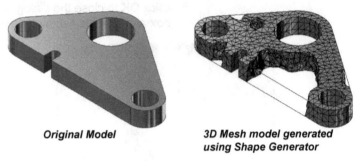

Original Model   *3D Mesh model generated using Shape Generator*

Figure 8–9

Promote the 3D Mesh Model

Once the mesh model has been generated, it can be promoted to the modeling environment to be used as a guide for making modeling changes to the geometry. In the Export panel, click

(Promote Shape) and select whether to copy the 3D mesh model directly to the part modeling environment (**Current Part File**) or to an STL file (**STL File**) that can be imported separately. Once the 3D mesh model displays, in the part modeling environment, you can use it as a guide to remove material from the part geometry.

Figure 8–10 shows an example of the promoted 3D mesh model in the part modeling environment and the final geometry based on suggested areas to be removed.

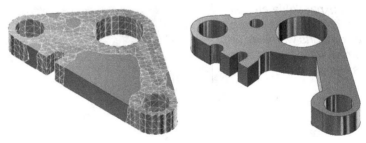

3D Model Promoted to the Part Modeling Environment   *Final Solid Geometry*

Figure 8–10

Consider the following when using a 3D mesh model to make changes to your design:

- When making geometry changes to the model, consider using lines and arcs where possible to help ensure that the final geometry is manufacturable.

- Not all geometry needs to be removed. This is a recommendation based on the criteria set.

The constraints and loads set in Shape Generator can be reused in the Stress Analysis environment.

- Consider using the Stress Analysis environment to further analyze the structural integrity of the final geometry.

Hint: Visual Style

Consider using the Wireframe visual style when using the 3D mesh model to make design changes. This enables you to see how the mesh model looks inside the solid geometry.

Practice 8a

Generating a Design using Shape Generator

Practice Objectives

- Create a Shape Generator study that sets a goal to meet a mass reduction target.
- Assign material, constraint, and load criteria in a Shape Generator study to accurately define a model's working environment.
- Set regions in the model that will not be removed after the Shape Generator study is complete.
- Define a symmetry plane in the model.
- Promote a Shape Generator study to the modeling environment.

In this practice, you will open a model that represents the overall shape and volume of an actuator mounting block that exists in a top-level assembly. The Shape Generator tool will be used to suggest modeling changes that helps to reduce the mass of the model to under 3 lbs. You will define the material, constraints, loads, preserved regions, and a symmetry plane prior to running the study. Figure 8–11 shows the model's progress through the practice.

 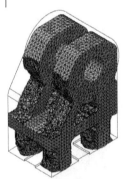 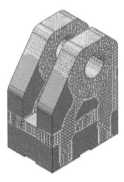 

Original Geometry *Analyzed 3D Mesh* *Promoted Shape Geometry* *Modified Solid Geometry*

Figure 8–11

Task 1 - Open an existing part model in the Shape Generator environment.

1. Open **Actuator Block.ipt** from the practice files folder.

2. In the *3D Model* tab> Explore panel, click (Shape Generator).

3. Click **OK** if prompted with the Shape Generator dialog box. This provides an introduction to the tool and the option to access Help documentation. If this was previously disabled, you will not be shown this dialog box.

4. The *Analysis* tab becomes the active tab and the model and Model Browser display as shown in Figure 8–12. Set the model display as **Shaded with Hidden Edges** to better visualize the interior of the model, if not already set. The overall shape of the model was created using the part modeling features.

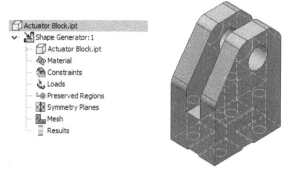

Figure 8–12

Task 2 - Define the material specification.

1. In the Material panel, click (Assign) to open the Assign Materials dialog box, as shown in Figure 8–13.

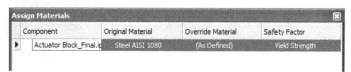

Figure 8–13

2. Maintain the **(As Defined)** option in the Override Material drop-down list. This uses the material that was defined when the model was created.

3. Click **OK**.

Task 3 - Apply constraints and loads that will represent the stresses that the part will encounter.

Pin constraints prevent faces from moving or deforming in combinations of radial, axial, or tangential directions

1. In the *Analysis* tab>Constraints panel, click ◯ (Pin).

2. Ensure that the ⬚ (Location) button is active and select the cylindrical surface shown in Figure 8–14.

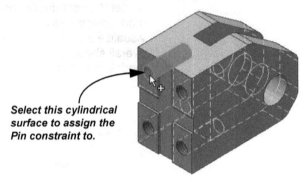

Select this cylindrical surface to assign the Pin constraint to.

Figure 8–14

3. Click **Apply** to assign the constraint and leave the dialog box open. The Pin glyph displays on the model.

4. Continue to apply three additional Pin constraints to the remaining 3 support holes on the bottom of the model. Once assigned, the model and Model Browser should display as shown in Figure 8–15.

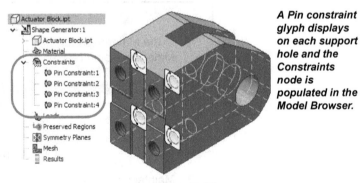

A Pin constraint glyph displays on each support hole and the Constraints node is populated in the Model Browser.

Figure 8–15

5. Click **Cancel** to close the dialog box.

6. Change the view display to **Shaded** if you had been working in an alternate view style.

7. In the *Analysis* tab>Loads panel, click ⊙ (Bearing).

8. Ensure that the ☐ (Faces) button is active and select the two cylindrical faces shown in Figure 8–16 as the reference faces to which the **Bearing** load is being assigned (blue faces).

9. By default, the load is along the axis of the cylinder and the direction of the load is radial. Click ☐ in the *Direction* area and select the face shown in Figure 8–16 as the direction reference (green face). A glyph displays on the model indicating the direction in which the load is applied.

To assign the load based on the vector directions, expand the dialog box and enter the values in the additional fields that are provided.

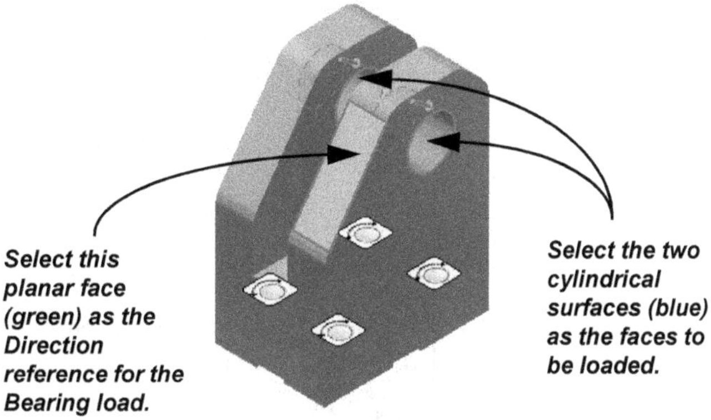

Select this planar face (green) as the Direction reference for the Bearing load.

Select the two cylindrical surfaces (blue) as the faces to be loaded.

Figure 8–16

10. Set the load *Magnitude* to **5000 N**, as shown in Figure 8–17.

Figure 8–17

11. Click ⬚>> on the dialog box to access the additional settings. Enter **Bearing** as the custom name for the load.

12. Click **OK** to assign the load and close the dialog box. The **Bearing** load has been added to the **Loads** node in the Model Browser.

Task 4 - Define the Shape Generator Settings.

The current mass of the model is 4.51 Lbs. The design goal in this model is to reduce the weight to under 3 lbs.

1. To open the Shape Generator Settings dialog box, click
    ⬚ (Shape Generator Settings).

2. Select **Target Mass** and enter **2.99lbmass**, as shown in Figure 8–18.

3. Maintain the *Mesh Resolution* slider at **3.000**, as shown in Figure 8–18.

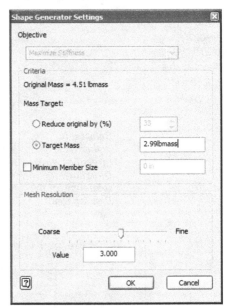

Figure 8–18

4. Click **OK**.

Task 5 - Set zones that will be preserved

1. In the Goals and Criteria panel, click ⬚ (Preserve Region).

2. In the Preserve Region dialog box, click ⬚ and select one of the cylindrical faces that was used in placing the **Bearing** load.

3. The Preserve Region dialog box updates to create a cylindrical region. Use the arrows on the various sides of the cylindrical bounding box to drag it, as shown in Figure 8–19. Ensure that the preserved area extends the width of the part and preserves the material above and around the holes.

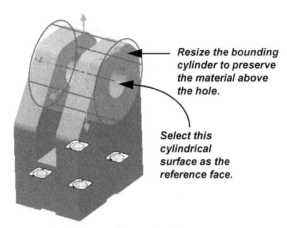

Resize the bounding cylinder to preserve the material above the hole.

Select this cylindrical surface as the reference face.

Figure 8–19

4. Click **OK**.

5. Reorient the model to the **BOTTOM** view using the ViewCube.

6. In the Model Browser, expand the **Constraints** node. Right-click on **Pin Constraint1** and clear the **Visibility** option, as shown in Figure 8–20. This removes the glyph from the model display.

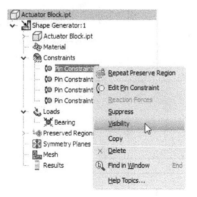

Figure 8–20

7. Clear the glyph display for the other three Pin constraints.

8. In the Goals and Criteria panel, click 🖰 (Preserve Region).

9. Ensure that 🖰 is active and select the edge of the circular hole, as shown in the BOTTOM view in Figure 8–21.

10. Click ⟩⟩ to expand the dialog box. In the *Region Dimensions* area, set the *Radius* value to **0.4 in** and the *Length* value to **1.1 in**. Ensure that the length is extending into the model, as shown in the FRONT view in Figure 8–21. In the *Center Point* area, set the *Y* value to **.55in**. Click **Apply**.

Select this circular edge as the reference for the Preserved Region.

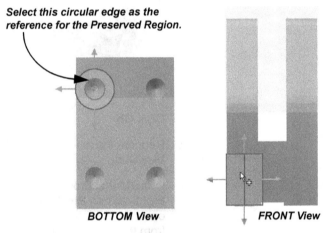

BOTTOM View   FRONT View

Figure 8–21

11. Create three identical preserved regions on the other support holes. The model should display as shown in Figure 8–22.

Figure 8–22

One additional preserve area is required to ensure that material is not removed that will affect the stability along the X axis.

12. Click  (Preserve Region), if the dialog box is not already open.

13. Select the planar face that connects the two symmetric sides. Using the ViewCube, reorient the model to size the bounding box similar to that shown in Figure 8–23. The box should extend the width of the model and extend into the preserve areas for the support holes. Click **OK** to create the preserved area.

Select this planar face to place the bounding box.   *Resize the bounding box to create this preserved area.*

Figure 8–23

14. All six preserved areas are listed in the **Preserved Regions** node in the Model Browser.

Task 6 - Define symmetry in the model.

The model is symmetric about the YZ plane. This should be assigned as criteria to ensure that the 3D mesh model is symmetric.

1. In the Goals and Criteria panel, click (Symmetry Plane).

2. By default, the symmetry planes are placed at the center of mass and are aligned with the global coordinate system. No change is required to reposition the planes for this model.

3. Toggle the active planes so that the YZ plane is the only plane highlighted in red, as shown in Figure 8–24.

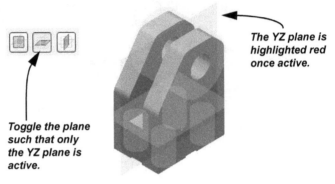

Toggle the plane such that only the YZ plane is active.

The YZ plane is highlighted red once active.

Figure 8–24

4. Click **OK** to assign the symmetry plane.

5. Save the model.

Task 7 - Run the Shape Generator and promote the study.

Now that the analysis has been setup, you can run the shape generator and promote the study to the model environment.

1. Click (Generate Shape) to open the Generate Shape dialog box.

The analysis may take a few minutes to complete. The run time will vary depending on your computer.

Additionally, warnings may be presented as the geometry is optimized.

2. Click **Run** to start the shape generator analysis.

3. Once complete, a 3D mesh should display similar to that shown in Figure 8–25.

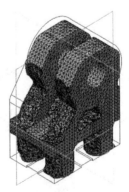

Figure 8–25

4. In the Export panel, click 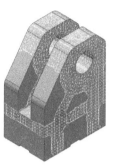 (Promote Shape) and select **Current Part File** to promote the optimized 3D mesh directly to the part model. Click **OK**.

5. Click **OK** in the Promote Shape dialog box that displays. This dialog box, indicates that shape promotion was successful and provides recommended steps. The 3D mesh displays embedded in the solid geometry, as shown in Figure 8–26.

Figure 8–26

Task 8 - Modify the initial design using the Shape Generator's 3D mesh.

If time permits, try to create the sketches in your own model.

1. Open **Actuator Block_Final.ipt**. This model already has been optimized using Shape Generator and sketches that approximate the material removal have been created for you.

2. Using the **Side Cut Profiles** and **Front Cut Profile** sketches, create the geometry shown in Figure 8–27.

Figure 8–27

3. Open the model's iProperties dialog box and update its physical properties. Note that the mass is still slightly over 3lbs.

4. To further reduce the mass of the model, you can add fillets to the edges of the geometry, modify the sketches that were used to remove the material, and/or change to a lower weight steel. Ultimately, the changes that are made must still be analyzed for structural integrity to ensure it can withstand its loads; however, the Shape Generator has provided a satisfactory starting point.

5. Save the model and close the window.

Chapter Review Questions

1. The Shape Generator tool automatically modifies the initial geometry of the model when it is promoted to the part modeling environment.

    a. True

    b. False

2. In which Autodesk Inventor working environment can you gain access to the Shape Generator tool? (Select all that apply.)

    a. Part Modeling

    b. Assembly Modeling

    c. Drawing

    d. Presentation

    e. Stress Analysis

3. Only a single shape generation study can be setup in a model.

    a. True

    b. False

4. Which of the following constraints can be added to the model to accurately describe how it is constrained in its working environment? (Select all that apply.)

    a. **Bearing**

    b. **Fixed**

    c. **Force**

    d. **Frictionless**

    e. **Gravity**

    f. **Moment**

    g. **Pin**

    h. **Pressure**

5. Which of the following cannot be controlled using the additional options in the expandable load creation dialog boxes? (Select all that apply.)

   a. The location reference of the load.

   b. The direction reference for a load.

   c. The magnitude of the load broken down into vector components.

   d. The assignment of a custom load name.

   e. The display of the load glyph in the model.

   f. The scale of the load glyph when it displays in the model.

6. Which of the following are valid when setting the criteria for a Shape Generator analysis? (Select all that apply.)

   a. The volume of the model is set to reach a target value.

   b. The mass of the model is set to reach a target value.

   c. The volume of the model is reduced by a set percentage value.

   d. The mass of the model is reduced by a set percentage value.

7. A cylindrical face that is selected as the reference for a preserved region cannot use the **Box** option to define its boundary.

   a. True

   b. False

8. How many planes can be selected during a Shape Generator analysis to define symmetry in a model?

   a. 1

   b. 2

   c. 3

   d. Unlimited

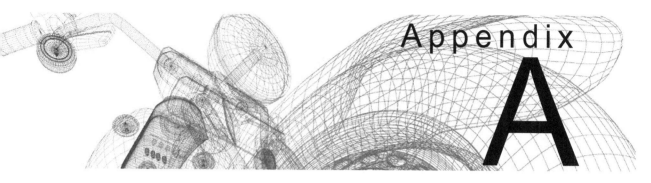

Sheet Metal Enhancements

In this chapter, you learn about the new enhancements that have been introduced into the Sheet Metal environment with the Autodesk® Inventor® 2016 and 2017 software releases. The main focus is on the ability to incorporate a multi-body modeling design strategy for creating sheet metal models. Additionally, you will learn how to improve modeling efficiency using new corner relief options, the various changes to how punches display in flat patterns, the support for zero bend radius features, and how to defer flat pattern updates.

Learning Objective in this Chapter

- Create a multi-body sheet metal part file that represents multiple assembly components in a single file.
- Use bodies to create individual sheet metal part files.
- Describe the various enhancements incorporated to ease sheet metal feature creation.

A.1 Multi-Body Modeling

Creating sheet metal parts using a multi-body modeling workflow enables you to create your entire assembly design in the part environment using both sheet metal and 3D modeling feature commands. The design is arranged into separate bodies in a single sheet metal part file. Figure A–1 shows a model that has five solid bodies. **Solid3** is expanded in the Model Browser to display the features that were used to create this solid. Each of these separate bodies can then be extracted into individual parts for a new assembly.

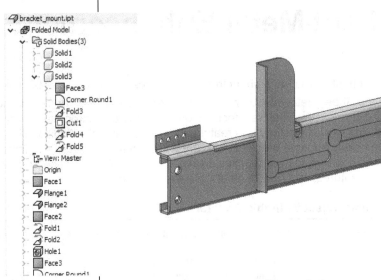

Figure A–1

The advantages of building a file using multi-bodies include the following:

- You do not need to create an initial complex file and directory structure to design parts in the context of a top-level assembly. The entire design resides in a single file and bodies are later extracted to create parts.

- A complex part file can be better organized using separate bodies with respect to their function or position in the model.

- Relationships between bodies can be set up and broken.

- You can control the visibility of bodies as a group rather than at the individual feature level.

All sheet metal models contain a *Solid Bodies* folder in the Model Browser. This folder lists all solids in the part. For the model in Figure A–2, the *Solid Bodies* folder contains three solids.

Figure A–2

Hint: Use Sheet Metal Styles and Thickness

When designing sheet metal models using the multi-body modeling technique, it is recommended that you drive the model's thickness using the Sheet Metal Rule. This helps to ensure that when the bodies are extracted to create their own part files that the thickness values match the style of the newly created model and that the model can be flattened. If the values differ, the model cannot be unfolded.

Creating the First Solid Body

With the creation of the first feature in any sheet metal file, the first solid body is automatically created. This is because

(New Solid) is automatically selected in the feature creation dialog box, as shown in Figure A–3. Once the base feature is created, the *Solid Bodies* folder displays in the Model Browser and the first solid body is added to the folder.

Figure A–3

Creating Additional Solid Bodies

Once the first solid body is added to the model, each additional feature is automatically applied to it, unless a new feature is explicitly set to be created as a new solid body. To create a new solid body, create its feature as you normally would, but click

⌞ (New Solid) in the feature creation dialog box or in the mini-toolbar. Once selected, a second body is added.

Assigning Features to Solid Bodies

Once two or more solid bodies are in a model, the selection of the placement/sketch planes are important to correctly locate the new feature on to the required solid body. Consider the following:

- When creating a sketched feature, it is by default added to the same solid body as that of the sketch plane. For features to be added to a different solid body, click ⌞ (Solids) in the feature dialog box and then select the required solid body.

- When creating a pick-and-place feature, it is by default added to the same solid body as the placement references. In the case of a Corner Round, for example, it is added to the same solid body as the parent feature of the placement edge. If multiple edges are selected that belong to multiple solid bodies, the feature is added to each solid body.

- When creating a sketch-based or pick-and-place feature, it is only extended through its parent solid body, even if the **Through All** depth option is selected. For features to interact with another solid body, click ⌞ (Solids) in the feature dialog box and then select additional solid bodies to be included.

Manipulating Solid Bodies

Once multiple solid bodies exist in the model, you can further manipulate them. You can redefine them as part of another solid body, move them, split them, and combine them.

Redefining/Removing Features in Solid Bodies

Once a feature is created and assigned to a solid body, you can re-assign it to another solid body or remove a solid body from interacting with the feature. To do so, redefine the original feature and click ⌞ (Solids) to activate it. You can select the new solid to apply it to or, if you want to remove a solid body from the initial selection set, press and hold <Ctrl> and select the solid body to remove.

Moving Bodies

You might need to move the various bodies in a multi-body part.

*The **Move** command is only available when working with solid bodies.*

How To: Move a Solid Body

1. In the *3D Model* tab>expanded Modify panel, click ⬚ (Move Bodies). The Move Bodies dialog box opens.
2. Select the solid bodies to move. If you need to select multiple bodies, you must click ⬚ (Bodies) again after selecting the first body to select additional bodies.
3. Select a move operation using the drop-down list in the Move Bodies dialog box, as shown in Figure A–4.

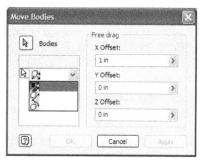

Figure A–4

Each icon in the list enables you to move the body, as follows:

- ⬚ (**Free drag**): Enables you to enter a precise X, Y, or Z offset value, or drag the preview in any direction.

- ⬚ (**Move along ray**): Enables you to enter a precise offset value, or drag the preview offset from a selected reference.

- ⬚ (**Rotate about line**): Enables you to enter a precise rotational angle value, or drag the preview around a selected axis.

4. Depending on the move operation selected, enter values and select references using the right side of the dialog box to define the movement.

5. To define a second move operation, if required, select **Click to add** and select a new move operation, as shown in Figure A–5.

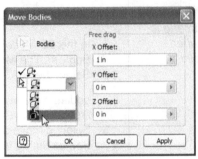

Figure A–5

6. Continue to add move operations as required.
7. Click **OK** to complete the feature. A Move Body feature is added to the bottom of the Model Browser, as well as into each of the Solid Bodies selected to be moved.

*To edit the Move Body feature, right-click on it and select **Edit feature**.*

Splitting Bodies

You can split a single body so that you can manipulate the resulting bodies independently.

How To: Split a Solid Body

*The **Split** command is available when working with solid bodies or Autodesk Inventor features.*

1. In the *3D Model* tab>Modify panel, click (Split).

2. Click (Split Solid) as the split method. The Split dialog box opens as shown in Figure A–6.

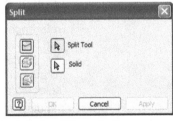

Figure A–6

3. Select a work plane or a sketch as the *Split Tool*. The split tool defines where the split occurs.
4. Select the Solid body to split. If a sketch was selected as the split tool, the solid body to which the sketch plane belongs is automatically selected as the solid to be split. You can reselect this reference, as required.
5. Click **OK** to complete the split.

Combining Bodies

If you created two solid bodies separately during an initial design, you might decide later that they should be combined. Using the **Combine** command, you can add or remove material based on selected bodies.

How To: Combine Features

*The **Combine** command is only available when working with solid bodies.*

1. In the *3D Model* tab>Modify panel, click 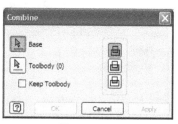 (Combine). The Combine dialog box opens as shown in Figure A–7.

Figure A–7

2. Select the solid body to use as the *Base* reference. The base body is the solid body on which the operation is going to be performed.

You can only select one base body, but you can select multiple toolbodies, if required.

3. Select the solid body to use as the *Toolbody* reference. The toolbody is the solid body or bodies that is going to perform the operation.
4. (Optional) To maintain the toolbody as a solid body after the operation, select **Keep Toolbody**. If you select this option, toolbody becomes invisible. This option is only available during the initial combine operation, not during the editing process.
5. Select an operation to perform on the base. The available operations include joining (), cutting (), and intersecting () the toolbody from the base.
6. Click **OK** to complete the feature. The Combine feature is listed at the bottom of the Model Browser and in the solid body used as the base reference.

Inserting Components into Parts

Using the **Derive** option, you can selectively include/exclude solid bodies (or other objects) from a source model to import it into a new or existing part file.

Creating Parts from Part Bodies

The steps for creating a part is similar to that for deriving a part.

You can extract individual bodies from a multi-body sheet metal part into separate sheet metal parts.

How To: Extract a Body to Create a New Sheet Metal Part

1. In the *Sheet Metal* tab>Flat Pattern panel, click (Make Part). Alternatively, you can right-click on a Solid Body in the Model Browser and select **Make Part**. The Make Part dialog box opens, as shown in Figure A–8.

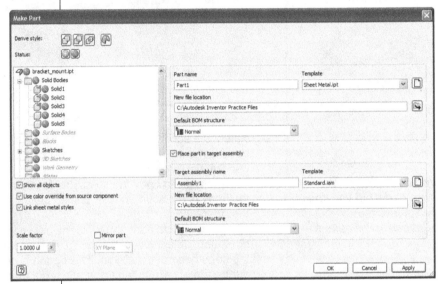

Figure A–8

2. Select a **Derive style** icon from the top of the dialog box to define how to create the component. The icons are described as follows:

Icon	Description
	Create single solid body where seams between planar faces as removed.
	Create single solid body where seams between planar faces are kept.
	Keep each solid as an individual solid body.
	Create the body as a work surface.

*Use the **Show all objects** option to refine the tree in the Make Part dialog box to either show all objects that can be included/excluded, or to only list those headings that have applicable data in the solid body.*

3. Enable or disable which portions (e.g., solid bodies, sketches, parameters, etc.) of the model to use to create the new part by toggling the **Status** icons adjacent to the item name. If the **Make Part** command was accessed from the Model Browser, the part selected will automatically be included.

   - A yellow circle with a plus symbol (⊕) indicates that the geometry is included in the new part.

   - A gray circle with a slash symbol (⊘) indicates that the geometry is not included in the new part.

   - A circle that is half yellow and half gray (◑) indicates that some geometry in the object type is included, while some is not.

4. Define the remaining options on the right side of the Make Part dialog box to fully define the new part (e.g., part name, template to use, etc.).

5. (Optional) If you require the part to be in a new assembly, select **Place part in target assembly** and enter the assembly information.

6. Click **OK** to complete the part. Depending on the *Derive style* selected, the new part might combine the selected bodies into a single body, or keep each body separate.

The newly created part remains associative to the multi-body part, unless you explicitly break the link. In the newly created part, right-click on the source part name that has been imported and select **Break Link With Base Component**. The link can be suppressed (instead of broken) by selecting **Suppress Link With Base Component**.

Creating Components from Part Bodies

Selected bodies in a multi-body part can be extracted into separate components that are combined in a new top-level assembly.

How To: Extract Solid Bodies and Create a New Assembly from Them

1. In the *Sheet Metal* tab>Flat Pattern panel, click 📐 (Make Components). The Make Components: Selection dialog box opens.

2. Select the solid bodies to extract in the Model Browser. All selected solid bodies are listed in the dialog box.

3. Ensure that the **Insert components in target assembly** option is selected.

4. Specify the remaining options on the right side of the Make Components: Selection dialog box to fully define the new component (e.g., target assembly name, template to use, etc.). The dialog box displays similar to that shown in Figure A–9 once components have been selected.

Consider using the **Make Component** *command and disabling the* **Insert components in target assembly** *option instead of using the* **Make Part** *command multiple times when creating more than one component from a multi-body part.*

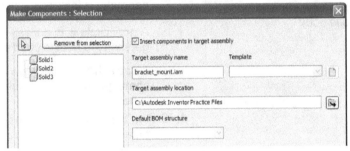

Figure A–9

5. Click **Next**. The Make Components: Bodies dialog box opens.

The solid body name in the source model is used as the default name for the component.

6. Using the Make Components: Bodies dialog box, you can make changes to individual components that are being created as part of the assembly. You can click in each column to rename the resulting component, or change its template or BOM Structure. The dialog box opens similar to that shown in Figure A–10.

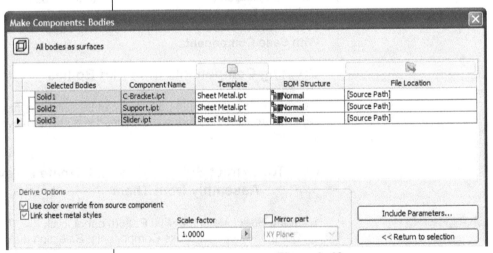

Figure A–10

7. Set the options in the *Derive Options* area, as required.
8. Click **OK** to complete the operation.

The newly created sheet metal parts and assembly remain associative to the multi-body part unless you explicitly break the link to the parent model. To break the link, you must open each created component, then right-click on the source part name that has been imported and select **Break Link With Base Component**. The link can be suppressed instead of broken by selecting **Suppress Link With Base Component**.

Solid Body Display

To control the visibility of a solid body, right-click on the solid body and enable or disable the **Visibility** option.

Solid Body Properties

To access the properties for a solid body, right-click on the solid body name and select **Properties**. The Body Properties dialog box opens as shown in Figure A–11.

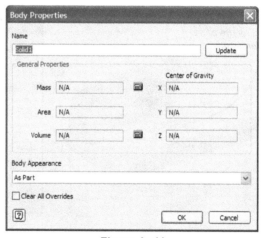

Figure A–11

Using the Body Properties dialog box, you can do the following:

*The **Clear All Overrides** option removes color overrides from individual faces contained in the solid body.*

- Rename the solid body. You can also rename a solid body directly in the Model Browser.

- Update and provide the general properties for the solid body.

- Set a color style for the solid body.

A.2 Miscellaneous Sheet Metal Enhancements

Thickness Detection

Prior to 2016, when converting part model geometry to a sheet metal model, you had to access the Sheet Metal Defaults dialog box to verify and/or change the default thickness for the sheet metal model. As of 2016, when you use the **Convert to Sheet Metal** ( ) option, you are prompted to select a base face reference on the geometry from which a measurement will be taken to populate the *Thickness* value. For the example shown in Figure A–12, the solid model on the left is being converted by selecting the indicated face. Once this face is selected, a measurement is automatically taken and the Sheet Metal Defaults dialog box opens and displays the measured *Thickness* value. Click **OK** to close the dialog box and continue working in the Sheet Metal environment.

This face was selected as the base face reference.

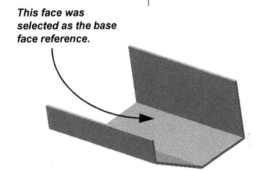

Figure A–12

Direct Edit

The **Direct** (Edit) command is now available for use in the Sheet Metal environment. To access this command, expand the Modify panel and select 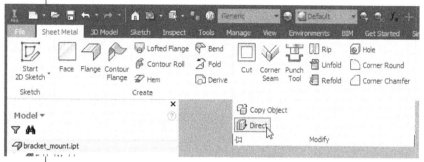 (Direct), as shown in Figure A–13. Direct Edit is a method of editing both imported data and native Autodesk Inventor parametric models. These tools enable you to delete and adjust the size, scale, shape, and location of features by directly manipulating geometry in the model.

Figure A–13

Corner Rounds & Corner Chamfers

Some dialog boxes (i.e. Corner Round) are now resizable.

Using the Autodesk Inventor 2017 (R1) software, it is now possible to use the **Apply** option in both the Corner Round or Corner Chamfer dialog boxes, as shown in Figure A–14. This option enables you to improve efficiency when creating these features, as you can apply the feature and continue to create additional ones without having to restart the command.

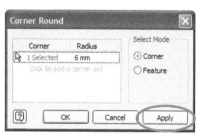

Figure A–14

Corner Relief

Additional placement solutions are now available when adding round or square corner reliefs into a model. Prior to Inventor 2017, the round and square corner relief types were placed at the intersection. It is now possible to define alternate placement options, as follows:

- A **Round** Corner Relief is a circular cut out in the flat pattern. It can be centered at the intersection of the bend lines, tangent to the adjacent flange edges, or positioned with its circumferences on the vertex, as shown on the left in Figure A–15. Refer to the images in the dialog boxes to preview how the *Relief Placement* options vary a round corner relief.

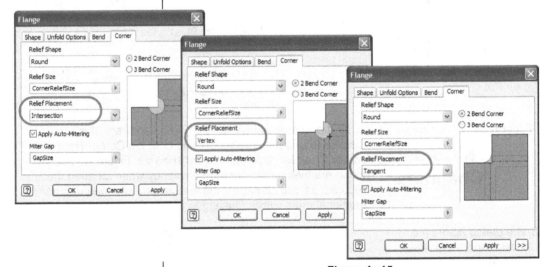

Figure A–15

- A **Square** Corner Relief is a square cut out in the flat pattern. It can be centered of the intersection of the bend lines, or positioned on the vertex, as shown on the right in Figure A–16. Refer to the images in the dialog boxes to preview how the *Relief Placement* options vary a square corner relief.

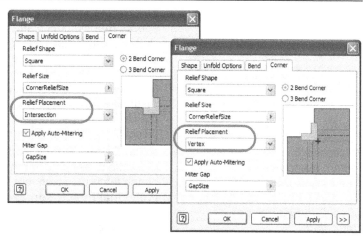

Figure A–16

Punch

The following enhancements have been introduced for the Punch Tool:

- With the release of the Autodesk Inventor 2017 (R1) software, additional options are now available in the Punch Tool dialog box, in the *Preview* tab, as shown in Figure A–17.

Figure A–17

*To access the Flat Pattern dialog box, right-click on the node in the Model Browser and select **Edit Flat Pattern Definition**.*

- The **Unfold in Flat Pattern** checkbox enables you to specify that the punch should be unfolded in the Flat Pattern. This is possible as long as the punch geometry can be unfolded (e.g., was created as standard sheet metal features) and it does not result in deformed shapes (e.g., louver geometry results in deformation and cannot be unfolded). Additionally, when the punch was created, the **Unfold in Flat Pattern** checkbox must have been select in the Extract iFeature dialog box.

- A **Flat Pattern Punch Representation** menu is now available to assign different representations for individual punch features. To enable this in a flat pattern, the **Ignore Individual Punch Representation Settings** checkbox in the *Punch Representation* tab, in the Flat Pattern dialog box must be cleared.

- In the *Geometry* tab, you can now easily identify the number of punch instances that will be added to the model, as shown in Figure A–18. Prior to 2016, the number of instances was not displayed.

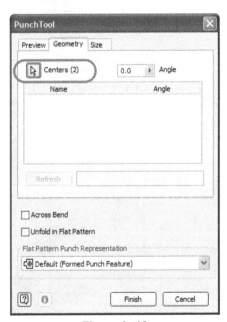

Figure A–18

Zero Bend Radius

As of 2016, you are now able to apply zero bend radius to the following commands:

- **Face**

- **Bend**

- **Flange**

- **Contour Roll**

- **Lofted Flange**

- **Hem**

- **Fold**

To assign a zero bend radius, simply enter a **0** value in the *Bend Radius* field, as shown on the right in Figure A–19.

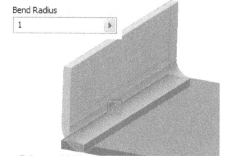

Prior to 2016 you could enter custom BendRadius values but couldn't enter a 0 value.

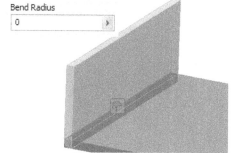

As of 2016 you can now enter 0 as a custom BendRadius value.

Figure A–19

Flat Patterns

Prior to 2017, when a flat pattern was created, it automatically updated with changes to the folded model. It it now possible to right-click on the **Flat Pattern** node in the Model Browser and select **Defer Update**, as shown in Figure A–20. If activated, the flat pattern will not update automatically. The icon on the **Flat Pattern** node in the Model Browser changes to , indicating that changes to the folded model were made and that the defer status should be disabled to update the flat pattern.

*Alternatively, you can also enable the **Defer Update** option on the Modeling tab in the Document Settings dialog box or when opening the file on the File Open Options dialog box.*

Figure A–20

Exporting DWG and DXF Files

When exporting a .DWG or .DXF flat pattern file, you are now provided with an a new *2D Geometry* option called **Trim Centerlines at Contour**, as shown in Figure A–21. This option is located in the *Geometry* tab in the Flat Pattern DWG/DXF Export Options dialog box. This option enables the automatic trimming of bend centerlines to the edge of the cut. Additionally, it enables the exported flat pattern file to be used by shop tools that do not permit a bend centerline to cross a hole in the bend.

*To open the Flat Pattern DWG/DXF Export Options dialog box, right-click the **Flat Pattern** node in the Model Browser, select **Save Copy As**, enter a name, select the DWG or DXF file format, and click **Save**.*

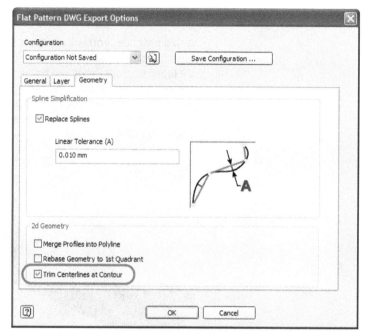

Figure A–21

- Any sketches included in the flat pattern will be exported with the properties specified in the Geometry Properties dialog box. Prior to Inventor 2017 (R2), the properties could not be exported.

Practice A1 | Multi-Body Sheet Metal Modeling

Practice Objectives

- Create multiple solid bodies in a single sheet metal part and modify and add features to specific bodies.
- Create a new assembly and part files by extracting solid bodies from the multi-body sheet metal part file.

In this practice, you will create a single sheet metal part file containing three solid bodies. In creating these solid bodies, you will learn to create multiple bodies in a model, add features to the bodies, and make required changes. To complete the practice you will use the multi-body model to create a top-level assembly and individual components for each body. The completed model is shown in Figure A–22.

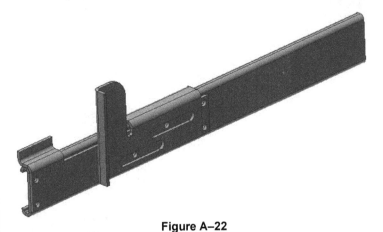

Figure A–22

Task 1 - Modify the bend radius for the flange features.

1. Open **multibody_bracket_mount.ipt** from the practice files folder. The model is a C-bracket and consists of a face and two flange features.

2. Zoom in on one of the ends of the model, as shown in Figure A–23.

3. In the Model Browser, double-click on **Flange1** to open its dialog box to make a change to the feature.

Prior to 2016, a zero bend radius was not possible.

4. In the *Bend Radius* field, note that the value is set to the default of **BendRadius**. Enter **0** as the new bend radius value and note how the model geometry updates, as shown in Figure A–24.

5. In the *Bend Radius* field, enter **BendRadius/2**. Note how the model geometry updates, as shown in Figure A–25.

Bend Radius = BendRadius

Figure A–23

Bend Radius = 0

Figure A–24

Bend Radius = BendRadius/2

Figure A–25

6. Click **OK** to complete the change.

7. Change the *Bend Radius* value for **Flange2** to **BendRadius/2**.

Task 2 - Create a second solid body in the model to represent a new sheet metal part.

1. Expand the **Solid Bodies** node in the Model Browser and note that there is a single Solid Body in the model, as shown in Figure A–26.

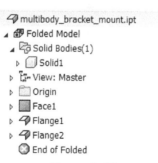

Figure A–26

2. In the Sheet Metal tab, click 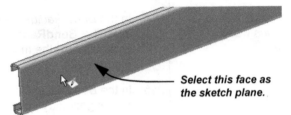 (Start 2D Sketch) and select the flat face shown in Figure A–27 as the new sketch plane.

Select this face as the sketch plane.

Figure A–27

3. Prior to sketching, ensure that the orientation of the model is similar to that shown in the ViewCube in Figure A–28. Orienting in this way ensures that the images and instructions in the following steps match.

4. Sketch and dimension the six linear entities shown in Figure A–28. The **.0625** dimension value is dimensioned to the projected edge of the bend on **Flange1**. The vertical edge on the left-hand side of the sketch is constrained to the projected Origin Center Point. Finish the sketch.

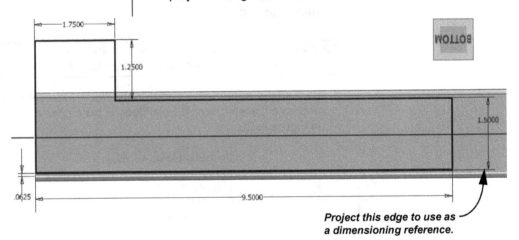

Project this edge to use as a dimensioning reference.

Figure A–28

5. In the *Sheet Metal* tab>Create panel, click 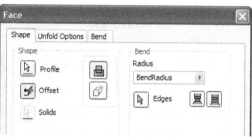 (Face). The Face dialog box opens, as shown in Figure A–29. By default, the new sketch is automatically selected as the Profile for the Face feature and a preview of the feature displays.

Figure A–29

6. In the *Shape* area, click 🖱️ (New Solid) to create the new feature as a solid in the model.

7. Click 🖱️ (Offset) to flip the feature so that the Face geometry is created away from the sketch plane. This ensures that the geometry in the two features does not intersect.

8. Click **OK** to create the new feature. The new geometry should display as shown in Figure A–30.

9. Expand the **Solid Bodies**, **Solid1**, and **Solid2** nodes in the Model Browser, as shown in Figure A–30. Note how the new **Face2** feature is only assigned to **Solid2**, while the other features are assigned to **Solid1**. The lower portion of the Model Browser lists all of the features in the order that they were created.

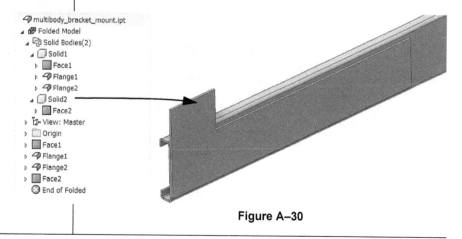

Figure A–30

10. Create a new sketch to define the bendline for a fold. Select the new face that was created as the sketch plane and sketch and dimension the line shown in Figure A–31. Ensure that the ends of the sketch are constrained using the **Coincident** constraint to the edges of the solid geometry.

Select this face as the sketch plane.

Project this edge to use as a dimensioning reference.

Sketch this horizontal line and dimension it from the projected edge.

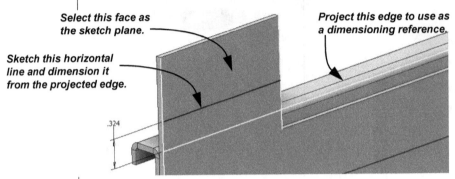

Figure A–31

11. Modify the offset dimension in the sketch to **.01** and complete the sketch.

12. In the *Sheet Metal* tab>Create panel, click ⟋ (Fold). Select the sketched line that was just created as the Bend Line reference. Use the *Flip Controls* are required to create the fold as shown in Figure A–32.

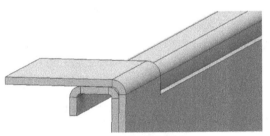

Figure A–32

13. Create the additional fold shown in Figure A–33.

Ensure that the bendline's sketch fully extends along the width of the geometry that will be folded.

Create this fold by sketching a bendline that is .45 in from its unbent edge.

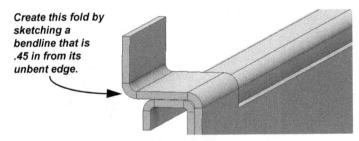

Figure A–33

14. Create the four sketch points in a new sketch on the face of **Solid2**. Project the XY Plane and ensure that the points are symmetric about this plane. Dimension and further constrain (points align horizontally and vertically) the sketch points so that the three dimensions shown in Figure A–34 fully constrain the sketch.

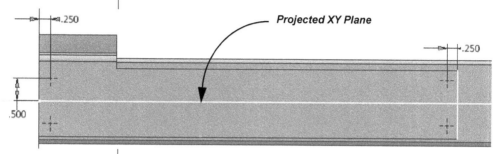

Figure A–34

15. Finish the sketch.

16. In the *Sheet Metal* tab>Modify panel, click 🔘 (Hole).

17. The four sketched points are automatically selected as references to place the holes. Enter **.25 in** as the diameter and select **Through All** as the *Termination* option. Click **OK**.

18. Spin the model and note that the holes, by default, only extrude through **Solid 2**. **Solid2** is automatically included because it is the parent of the sketch plane that was used to create the sketch points for the holes.

19. Edit **Hole1**. In the *Placement* area, select 🔲 (Solids) and select **Solid1** in the Model Browser or directly in the graphics window. Click **OK**.

20. Note that the holes now extrude through both solids.

21. Expand the **Solid Bodies** node in the Model Browser and note that the **Hole1** feature is now listed in both solids.

Task 3 - Create a third solid body in the model.

1. In the *Sheet Metal* tab, click 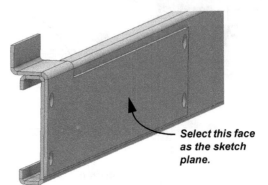 (Start 2D Sketch) and select the flat face shown in Figure A–35 as the new sketch plane.

Select this face as the sketch plane.

Figure A–35

2. Sketch and dimension the 9 entities shown in Figure A–36. The **.0625** dimension value is dimensioned to the projected edge of **Face2**. The vertical edge on the left-hand side of the sketch is constrained to the projected Origin Center Point.

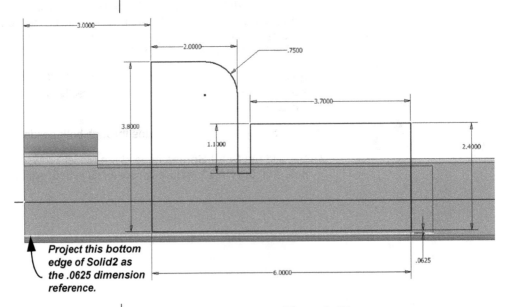

Project this bottom edge of Solid2 as the .0625 dimension reference.

Figure A–36

3. Finish the sketch.

4. In the *Sheet Metal* tab>Create panel, click ☐ (Face). The new sketch is automatically selected as the Profile.

5. In the *Shape* area, click 🖉 (New Solid) to create the new feature as a solid in the model.

6. Click 🖉 (Offset) to flip the feature so that the Face geometry is created away from the sketch plane to ensure that the geometry does not intersect.

7. Click **OK** to create the new feature.

8. Create the fold, corner round, and slotted cut features shown in Figure A–37. The slotted cuts can be created as either a single feature or individual features.

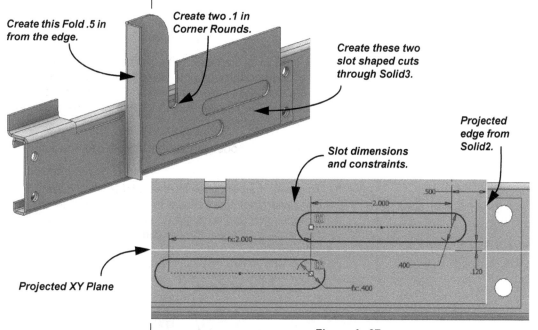

Figure A–37

Task 4 - Complete the model by adding holes and folds.

1. Create a new sketch on the face of **Solid2**.

2. Sketch the two points shown in Figure A–38. Center the points vertically in the slots and dimension them horizontally from the right-hand edge of **Solid2**.

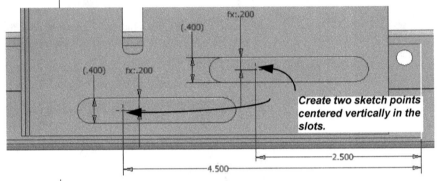

Create two sketch points centered vertically in the slots.

Figure A–38

3. Create two **.25 in** diameter holes on the two sketch points so that they extrude through both **Solid2** and **Solid1**. These holes are required to position rivets that will connect all three components and enables **Solid3** to slide. The rivets are not created in this practice.

4. To complete the model, create the two bends shown in Figure A–39.

   - To create the bendlines for these folds, sketch and dimension their lines similar to how the bendline was dimensioned and constrained in the fold shown in Figure A–31. Project the bendlines in **Solid1** as references.

Create two folds to bend Solid3 around Solid1.

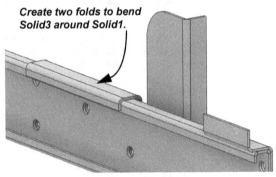

Figure A–39

5. Save the model. If you did not successfully complete the modeling in this practice, **multi_bracket_mount_FINAL.ipt** has been provided in the practice files folder to use to continue the next task.

Task 5 - Make components from the three solid bodies.

1. In the *Sheet Metal* tab>Flat Pattern panel, click 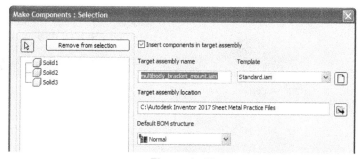 (Make Components). The Make Components: Selection dialog box opens.

2. Expand the **Solid Bodies** node in the Model Browser and select the three solid bodies. All selected solid bodies are listed in the dialog box, as shown in Figure A–40.

Figure A–40

3. Ensure that the **Insert components in target assembly** option is selected so that an assembly is automatically created for this model.

4. Specify the remaining options on the right side of the Make Components: Selection dialog box.

   - Assign the **Standard (in).iam** standard English assembly template.
   - Ensure that the *Target assembly* location is **C:\Autodesk Inventor 2017 Sheet Metal Practice Files**.
   - Accept the default assembly name and BOM structure.

5. Click **Next**. The Make Components: Bodies dialog box opens.

The solid body name in the source model is used as the default name for the component. As an alternative, you can also rename the solid bodies in the part file prior to making components.

6. Using the Make Components: Bodies dialog box, you can make changes to individual components that are being created as part of the assembly.

- Select each cell in the *Component Name* column to rename the new components that will be created. Use the names shown in Figure A–41.

- Select a cell in the *Template* column and select [□] at the top of the column. In the Open Template dialog box, select the *English* folder and select **Sheet Metal (in).ipt** as the default template to use. Assign this template to the other two models, as shown in Figure A–41.

- Ensure that the **Link sheet metal styles** option is selected to ensure that the thickness is correctly communicated to the new models. If this option is not selected, the sheet metal thicknesses might not match between the files and would prevent correct unfolding.

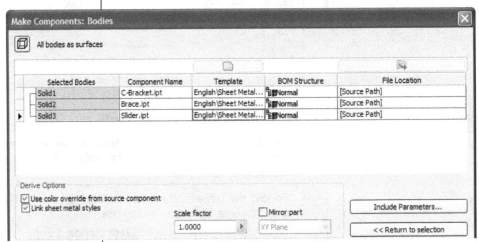

Figure A–41

7. Click **OK** to complete the operation. A new assembly model is created, as shown in Figure A–42.

Model ▾

▽ ⬩Assembly View ▾ 🔍

🗐 **multibody_bracket_mount.iam**

  ▢ Relationships

▷ 📇 Representations

▷ ▢ Origin

▷ ✏ C_Bracket:1

▷ ✏ Brace:1

▷ ✏ Slider:1

Figure A–42

8. Save the assembly and the models that were generated from the multi-body part model.

Task 6 - Open the C-Bracket component and create a flat pattern.

---

1. Right-click on the C-Bracket model in the assembly Model Browser and select **Open**.

2. In the *Sheet Metal* tab>Flat Pattern panel, click (Create Flat Pattern). The flat pattern displays.

3. Select the *multibody_bracket_mount.ipt* tab in the graphics window to return to the original multi-body sheet metal model. If you used the provided model to make the components, select the *multibody_bracket_mount_FINAL.ipt* tab instead.

4. Edit the sketch that was used to create **Face1**. Change the length of the sketch from **24 in** to **18 in**. Finish the sketch.

5. Return to the *C-Bracket.ipt* tab in the graphics window.

6. In the Quick Access toolbar, click (Local Update). Note that the geometry updates in the **C-Bracket.ipt** part to reflect the change in length.

Hint: Associativity

The newly created sheet metal parts and assembly remain associative to the multi-body part unless you explicitly break the link to the parent model.

To break the link, you must open each created component, right-click on the source part name that has been imported, and select **Break Link With Base Component**, as shown in Figure A–43.

The link can be suppressed (instead of broken) by selecting **Suppress Link With Base Component**.

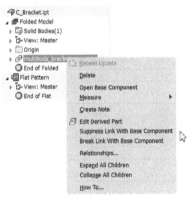

Figure A–43

Task 7 - Change the model thickness.

---

1. Select the *multibody_bracket_mount.ipt* tab in the graphics window to return to the original multi-body sheet metal model. If you used the provided model to make the components, select the *multibody_bracket_mount_FINAL.ipt* tab instead.

2. In the *Sheet Metal* tab>Setup panel, click (Sheet Metal Defaults).

3. Click (Edit Sheet Metal Rule) for the Sheet Metal Rule.

4. In the Style and Standard Editor, enter **0.125 in** as the new *Thickness* value, as shown in Figure A–44. Click **Save and Close**.

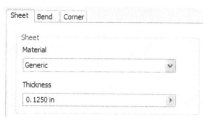

Figure A–44

5. Click **Cancel** to close the Sheet Metal Defaults dialog box. Note that the thickness of the model is updated and that all of the geometry reflects the change.

Consider conducting an interference analysis in the assembly to ensure that components do not interfere. Changes can then be made in the model and all other components update to reflect the change.

6. Select the *multibody_bracket_mount.iam* tab in the graphics window to return to the sheet metal assembly model.

7. In the Quick Access toolbar, click 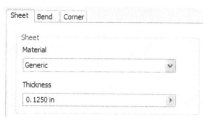 (Local Update). Note that the geometry updates to the new thickness.

   • If the model fails, consider reviewing the bendlines that were created in the model and ensure that the linear sketches are fully constrained coincidentally with the edges of the model.

8. Save the model and close all windows.

Chapter Review Questions

1. Multi-body part design requires the use of an assembly. Parts are created within the context of the assembly.

   a. True

   b. False

2. Each solid body in a multi-body sheet metal model can have a different *Thickness* value.

   a. True

   b. False

3. How are the second and any subsequent solid bodies created in a model?

   a. Explicitly set a new feature to be created as a new solid body.

   b. Each new feature is automatically added as a new solid body.

   c. Use specific solid body commands in the ribbon prior to creating the feature.

   d. None of the above.

4. Which of the following buttons/options is used in the Cut dialog box to ensure that the cut extrudes through multiple solid bodies?

   a.

   b.

   c.

   d. **Through All** (extent option)

5. Which solid body manipulation option enables you to create a single solid body from two solid bodies?

   a. Union

   b. Combine

   c. Extrude

   d. Split

6. A single Corner Round feature has been added to a model that currently has three solid bodies. An edge from each of the three solid bodies is selected as placement references. Which of the following statements is true regarding the model?

   a. A fourth solid body will be added to the model.

   b. The Corner Round feature will be added to the solid body in which the first reference edge belongs.

   c. The Corner Round feature will be added to each of the three solid bodies.

   d. The Corner Round feature will cause the three solid bodies to combine into one.

7. How is the thickness of a sheet metal part calculated when it is created by converting a standard part model?

   a. When converting, you must select the base feature. Its extruded depth is automatically assigned.

   b. When converting you must select a base face on the model. Based on this reference, a measurement of the thickness is automatically taken and assigned.

   c. This is not possible. You must assign the thickness using the Sheet Metal Rule.

8. Which of the following are valid Relief Placement options for a Square corner relief? (Select all that apply.)

   a. Intersection

   b. Vertex

   c. Tangent

9. Which of the following sheet metal features permit the entry of a zero bend radius value? (Select all that apply.)

   a. Face

   b. Flange

   c. Cut

   d. Hem

   e. Rip

   f. Fold

10. Once the **Defer Update** option is enabled for a Flat Pattern, changes to the folded model will automatically update in the flat pattern.

    a. True

    b. False

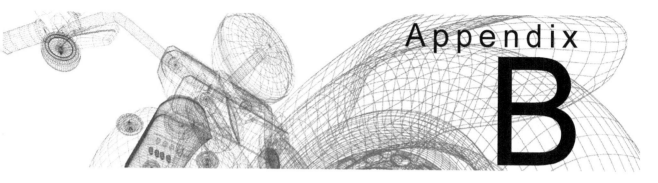

Appendix B

Inventor Studio Enhancements

Renderings help visualize a model's appearance before it is manufactured. You can apply different appearances, lighting styles, cameras, and local lights to create a realistic environment for the model. The overall workflow introduced in the Autodesk® Inventor® 2016 software is similar to previous versions; however, a new lighting style interface is now used to assign environments and a new rendering engine and options have been used.

Learning Objectives in this Chapter

- Assign a lighting style to an Inventor model to prepare it for rendering.
- Render a model in the Inventor Studio environment.

B.1 Studio Lighting Styles

Define the Studio Lighting Styles

In the Autodesk Inventor Studio environment (*Environments* tab> (Inventor Studio)), a new interface has been added in 2016 that enables you to assign a lighting style. In the Scene panel, click (Studio Lighting Styles). The Lighting Styles dialog box opens, as shown in Figure B–1. All of the new default lighting styles in Inventor Studio use Image-Based Lighting (IBL). They do not contain any local lights.

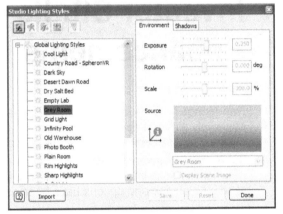

Figure B–1

- The Studio Lighting Styles dialog box lists the available lighting styles in two categories:
  - Global Lighting Styles are styles that are provided with the software.
  - Local Lighting Styles are styles that exist in the current file.

- A style must be listed in the Local Lighting Styles list to be used or modified for use in the model.

- Use any of the following methods to add a lighting style to the Local Lighting Styles list for use in the model:
  - Right-click on a Global Lighting Style and select **Active**.
  - Right-click on a Global Lighting Style and select **Copy Lighting Style** and enter a new name.
  - Right-click on a Global Lighting Style and select **New Lighting Style**.
  - Click (New Lighting Style) in the dialog box.

When activating or copying a lighting style to the local list, only the IBL environment is added. When using either of the **New Lighting Style** options, you are provided with the Grid Light IBL and three lights: directional, point, and spot. Each light has application default settings. By default, the directional, point, and spot lights are toggled off. You can toggle them on by changing individual light properties.

Directional, Point, and Spot lights are described as follows:

(Directional)	Simulates distant light sources, such as the sun. It has a direction, but no position. Directional light objects are symbolized in the model by an arrow, as shown. 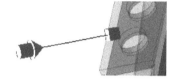
(Point)	Simulates a point source. It has a position and it radiates light in every direction. Point light objects are symbolized by an octahedron, as shown. 
(Spot)	Simulates a spot light with a position and direction. A Spot light emits light in the shape of a cone with two degrees of intensity. The most intense area is located within the inner area of the cone and the less intense area is located within the outer area of the cone of light. Spot light objects are symbolized by a cone, as shown. 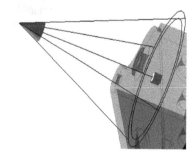

Adding Additional Lights

To create a new light in any selected lighting style, select the lighting style and click  (New Light). The Light dialog box opens, as shown in Figure B–2.

Figure B–2

Use the following tabs to define the lighting style:

- Use the *General* tab to define the type of light as Directional ( ), Point ( ), or Spot ( ). Select an edge or face as a target reference for the light, and then select a position along the reference line. Toggle the light on and off, and flip the direction of the light.

- Use the *Illumination* tab to adjust the intensity and color.

- Use the *Directional*, *Point*, or *Spot* tab to set options specific to the type of light that is selected. The tab name changes depending on the type of light being created. The options available in this tab enable you control the position and direction of the light as well as the light's specific properties.

Setting the Environment

Once a Global lighting style has been copied to the Local Lighting style list, you can edit the options on the *Environment* tab, as follows:

- To customize its exposure, rotation, and scale, modify the values or drag the scroll bar.

- Select the **Display Scene Image** option to display the image in the graphics window.

- To change the lighting style source image, select a new one using the drop-down list. If changed, any custom lights that were added are maintained.

Shadows

Use the *Shadows* tab to define the softness setting for the lighting style.

Saving Changes

Once you are finished adding additional lights, you can click **OK** to close the Light dialog box and return to the Studio Lighting Styles. Click **Save** to save any changes made to the lighting styles. When the required lighting effect has been achieved, save any changes and click **Done**.

B.2 Rendering

After defining the appropriate appearances, lighting styles, cameras, and local lights, you can render the image. In the Render panel, click 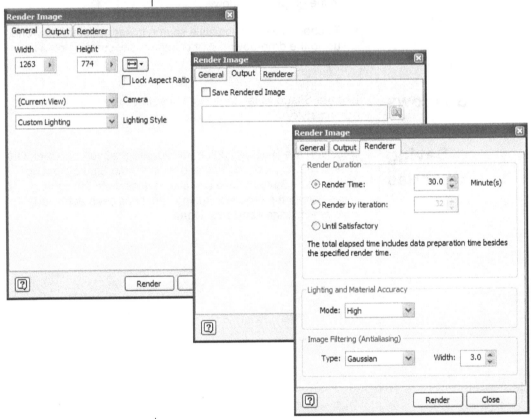 (Render Image). The three tabs that make up the Render Image dialog box are shown in Figure B–3.

Figure B–3

Use the following three tabs to define the options for rendering an image:

- Use the *General* tab to specify the width and height of the image you are rendering or use the **Output Size** menu. You can also lock the aspect ratio and specify the **Camera** and **Lighting Style**.

- If a new lighting style is assigned in the Lighting Style drop-down list, it is automatically added to the local list in the Studio Lighting Styles dialog box. Note that **Display Scene Image** cannot be enabled unless it is explicitly toggled on in the Studio Lighting Styles dialog box.

- Use the *Output* tab to specify whether or not to save the image once it is rendered. If saved, you can enter a name and location for the file.

  - The rendering can also be saved after rendering if this option was not set.

- Use the *Renderer* tab to control the render duration, accuracy of the lighting and materials that have been assigned, and the image filtering options to determine how accurate the rendering will be.

  - All three rendering options (**Render Time**, **Render by iteration**, and **Until Satisfactory**) enable you to restart the rendering once completed if it didn't produce a satisfactory result.

Once you have finished setting the rendering options, click **Render** to render the image. The Render Output window opens with the rendered image, as shown in Figure B–4.

Figure B–4

The rendering options for rendering an animation have been updated in a similar way.

Practice B1 | Rendering Images

Practice Objectives

- Apply an Appearance Override to individual parts in an assembly.
- Apply a lighting style to a model.
- Create a realistic rendered image.

In this practice, you will apply appearance overrides and a lighting style to an assembly model to render an image. The image shown in Figure B–5 is one of the images that you will create.

Figure B–5

Task 1 - Open an assembly file and apply appearance overrides.

1. Open **Vise.iam** from the *Vise_Inv_Studio_Assembly* folder.

2. In the Model Browser, select the **Screw_Sub:1** subassembly.

3. In the Quick Access toolbar, click (Appearance Browser) to open the Appearance Browser.

4. In the Appearance Browser, enter **Chrome** in the *Search* field at the top of the dialog box.

5. In the search results, select **Chrome - Polished**, and then right-click on it and select **Assign to Selection**. The material on the subassembly is now overridden and the Chrome - Polished material is now listed in the *Document Appearances* area.

6. Clear the *Search* field entry.

7. Clear the selection of the subassembly and select **Sliding_Jaw** and **Base** from the Model Browser.

8. Scroll down the list of materials, right-click on **Metal 1400F Hot**, and then select **Assign to Selection**. This material is assigned to the model and is copied to the *Document Appearances* area of the dialog box.

9. Close the Appearance Browser.

Task 2 - Set up the ground plane and set reflections.

1. In the *View* tab>Appearance panel, click **Ground Plane** to enable and display the ground plane in the graphics window.

*To adjust the ground plane location, expand the **Ground Plane** option in the Appearance panel and click **Settings**. In the Ground Plane Settings dialog box, ensure that the **Automatic adjustment to model** option is selected and enter a value in the Position & Size area to better position the plane.*

2. Click **Front** on the ViewCube. Note how the model is sitting on the ground plane. This should be verified to ensure that any reflections that are used when rendering are accurate.

3. Click **Ground Plane** to disable its display. The ground plane was only required to ensure the reflections will be correct when rendered.

4. Using the ViewCube return the model to the **Home** view.

5. In the *View* tab>Appearance panel, click **Reflections** to enable it. A reflection is now displayed in the graphics window.

Task 3 - Open the Inventor Studio Environment.

1. In the *Environments* tab>Begin panel, click 🫖 (Inventor Studio). The *Render* contextual tab displays.

2. The rendering will be the size of the graphics window. Zoom the model as required so that it uses the full size of the window.

3. In the Render panel, click ⬚ (Render Image). The Render Image dialog box opens, as shown in Figure B–6. By default, the current view and lighting is used for rendering.

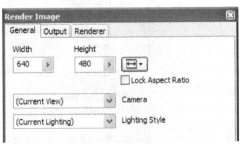

Figure B–6

4. Expand the Lighting Style drop-down list and select **Dark Sky**.

5. Expand the ⬚▾ drop-down list and select **Active View**. This sets the size of the rendered image to that of the current graphics window.

6. Select the *Renderer* tab. Change *Render Duration* to **Until Satisfactory** and leave the remaining defaults in the dialog box.

7. Click **Render**. The render will continue until you click

   ⬚ (Pause Rendering) in the top right-hand corner of the dialog box. The longer that you let the image render, the better quality of rendering you will get.

To automatically save an image once it is rendered, use the options on the Output tab. These options enable you to set a directory and file name for the file.

8. Once the image is rendered, click ⬚ (Save Rendering) in the Render Output window. In the Save dialog box, navigate to the *Vise_Inv_Studio_Assembly* folder and enter **Vise_Rendering1.bmp** as the name for the rendering. Click **Save**. The model shown in Figure B–7 was rendered for over six minutes.

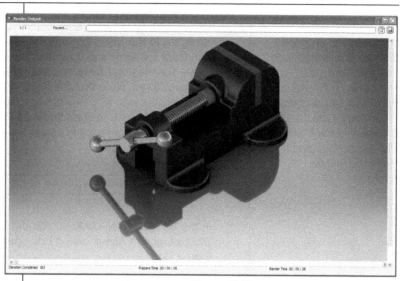

Figure B–7

9. Close the Render Output dialog box.

10. On the *General* tab, in the Lighting Style drop-down list, select **Warm Light**. This is a image-based lighting style that is provided with the software.

11. Render the image, which should display similar to that shown in Figure B–8. Save it as **Vise_Rendering2.bmp**.

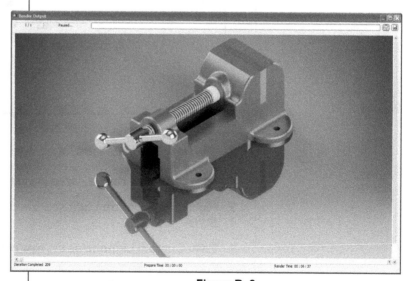

Figure B–8

If you did not complete the two renderings, two images (Vise_ Rendering1_Final.bmp and Vise_Rendering2 _Final.bmp) are provided in the Vise_ Inv_Studio_Assembly folder for you to compare.

12. Close the Render Output and Render Image dialog boxes.

13. Navigate to the *Vise_Inv_Studio_Assembly* folder in Windows Explorer and open the two saved images (**Vise_Rendering1.bmp** and **Vise_Rendering2.bmp**) to compare them. Note that the lighting in the second image is considerably warmer. This is because of the different image-based lighting style that was used. You will want to compare different styles to select the one that is best for your designs.

Task 4 - Working with a lighting style.

1. In the Scene panel, click ✶ (Studio Lighting Styles). The Studio Lighting Styles dialog box opens, as shown in Figure B–9.

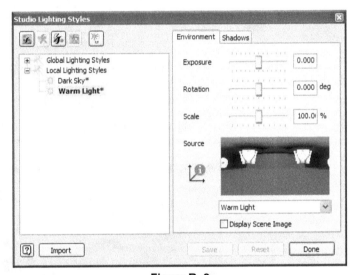

Figure B–9

2. The **Dark Sky** and **Warm Light** styles have been copied to the Local Lighting Styles area because they were used for rendering. They can be edited using the options, as required.

3. Right-click **on Warm Light** and select **Rename Lighting Style**.

4. Enter **Custom Lighting** as the new name and then click **OK**.

5. In the *Environment* tab, select **Display Scene Image** to show the gray background image of the style in the graphics window. Click **Save** to save the changes.

6. Right-click on **Custom Lighting** and note that **Active** is selected. Active styles are listed with their name displayed in bold font.

7. Click **Done** to close the dialog box.

   - Note that you cannot enable the scene image when assigning the lighting style in the Render Image dialog box. The image is only rendered with the lighting effects of the image.

8. In the Render panel, click 🫖 (Render Image). Ensure that the Lighting Style is set to the **Custom Lighting** style that was activated. Expand the ⊟▾ drop-down list and select **Active View**.

Vise_Rendering3_Final.bmp has been saved for you to review in the Vise_Inv_Studio_Assembly folder, if required.

9. Render the image and save it as **Vise_Rendering3.bmp**. Note that this rendering now has a gray background along with the warmer lights.

10. Close the Render Output and Render Image dialog boxes.

11. (Optional) Assign the **Empty Lab** lighting style using the Studio Lighting Styles dialog box by copying the style to the *Local Lighting Styles* area. Complete the following:

   - Locate the **Empty Lab** style in the *Global Lighting Styles* area. Right-click on the style, select **Copy Lighting Style**, and then enter a new name.
   - Set the new style as **Active**, if not already set.
   - Select **Display Scene Image** to show the style's background image in the graphics window.
   - Scale the background image to match the size of the model (approx. 36%).
   - Rotate the model, as required.
   - In the *View* tab, toggle off reflections and toggle on ground shadows.
   - Save the style and render the model.

A rendered version of the model is shown in Figure B–10.

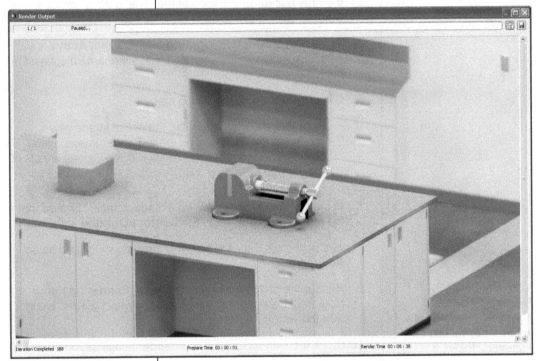

Figure B–10

12. Close the Render Output and Render Image dialog boxes.

13. Save the model and close the window.

Chapter Review Questions

1. When a Global Studio Lighting Style is assigned to the model, it is removed from the Global list of styles and moved to the Local list.

   a. True

   b. False

2. When using the (New Lighting Style) option in the Studio Lighting Styles dialog box, which of the following is the default Global Lighting Style that is assigned?

   a. Grid Light

   b. Gray Room

   c. Photo Booth

   d. Soft Light

   e. Warm Light

3. If a new lighting style is assigned in the Lighting Style drop-down list when it is being rendered, the scene display is automatically toggled on and used while rendering.

   a. True

   b. False

4. When rendering an image, where do you assign the file name for the rendered file before rendering begins?

   a. Render Image dialog box, *General* tab.

   b. Render Image dialog box, *Output* tab.

   c. Render Image dialog box, *Renderer* tab.

5. Which of the following three Rending Duration options enables you to stop and then restart a rendering if it is unsatisfactory? (Select all that apply.)

   a. **Render Time**

   b. **Until Satisfactory**

   c. **Render by iteration**

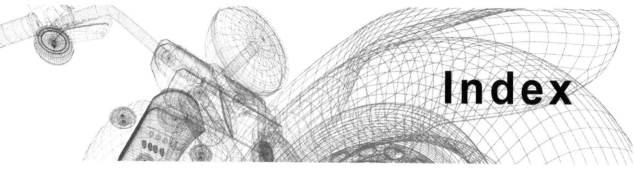

Index

www.ingramcontent.com/pod-product-compliance
Lightning Source LLC
Chambersburg PA
CBHW060526060326
40690CB00017B/3397